Mao: A Very Short Introduction

VERY SHORT INTRODUCTIONS are for anyone wanting a stimulating and accessible way in to a new subject. They are written by experts, and have been published in more than 25 languages worldwide.

The series began in 1995, and now represents a wide variety of topics in history, philosophy, religion, science, and the humanities. The VSI library now contains more than 300 volumes—a Very Short Introduction to everything from ancient Egypt and Indian philosophy to conceptual art and cosmology—and will continue to grow in a variety of disciplines.

Very Short Introductions available now:

ADVERTISING Winston Fletcher
AFRICAN HISTORY John Parker and Richard Rathbone
AGNOSTICISM Robin Le Poidevin
AMERICAN HISTORY Paul S. Boyer
AMERICAN IMMIGRATION David A. Gerber
AMERICAN POLITICAL PARTIES AND ELECTIONS L. Sandy Maisel
THE AMERICAN PRESIDENCY Charles O. Jones
ANAESTHESIA Aidan O'Donnell
ANARCHISM Colin Ward
ANCIENT EGYPT Ian Shaw
ANCIENT GREECE Paul Cartledge
ANCIENT PHILOSOPHY Julia Annas
ANCIENT WARFARE Harry Sidebottom
ANGELS David Albert Jones
ANGLICANISM Mark Chapman
THE ANGLO-SAXON AGE John Blair
THE ANIMAL KINGDOM Peter Holland
ANIMAL RIGHTS David DeGrazia
THE ANTARCTIC Klaus Dodds
ANTISEMITISM Steven Beller
ANXIETY Daniel Freeman and Jason Freeman
THE APOCRYPHAL GOSPELS Paul Foster
ARCHAEOLOGY Paul Bahn
ARCHITECTURE Andrew Ballantyne
ARISTOCRACY William Doyle
ARISTOTLE Jonathan Barnes
ART HISTORY Dana Arnold
ART THEORY Cynthia Freeland
ATHEISM Julian Baggini
AUGUSTINE Henry Chadwick

AUSTRALIA Kenneth Morgan
AUTISM Uta Frith
THE AVANT GARDE David Cottington
THE AZTECS David Carrasco
BARTHES Jonathan Culler
BEAUTY Roger Scruton
BESTSELLERS John Sutherland
THE BIBLE John Riches
BIBLICAL ARCHAEOLOGY Eric H. Cline
BIOGRAPHY Hermione Lee
THE BLUES Elijah Wald
THE BOOK OF MORMON Terryl Givens
BORDERS Alexander C. Diener and Joshua Hagen
THE BRAIN Michael O'Shea
BRITISH POLITICS Anthony Wright
BUDDHA Michael Carrithers
BUDDHISM Damien Keown
BUDDHIST ETHICS Damien Keown
CANCER Nicholas James
CAPITALISM James Fulcher
CATHOLICISM Gerald O'Collins
THE CELL Terence Allen and Graham Cowling
THE CELTS Barry Cunliffe
CHAOS Leonard Smith
CHILDREN'S LITERATURE Kimberley Reynolds
CHINESE LITERATURE Sabina Knight
CHOICE THEORY Michael Allingham
CHRISTIAN ART Beth Williamson
CHRISTIAN ETHICS D. Stephen Long
CHRISTIANITY Linda Woodhead
CITIZENSHIP Richard Bellamy

CIVIL ENGINEERING David Muir Wood
CLASSICAL MYTHOLOGY Helen Morales
CLASSICS Mary Beard and John Henderson
CLAUSEWITZ Michael Howard
THE COLD WAR Robert McMahon
COLONIAL AMERICA Alan Taylor
COLONIAL LATIN AMERICAN LITERATURE Rolena Adorno
COMEDY Matthew Bevis
COMMUNISM Leslie Holmes
THE COMPUTER Darrel Ince
THE CONQUISTADORS Matthew Restall and Felipe Fernández-Armesto
CONSCIENCE Paul Strohm
CONSCIOUSNESS Susan Blackmore
CONTEMPORARY ART Julian Stallabrass
CONTINENTAL PHILOSOPHY Simon Critchley
COSMOLOGY Peter Coles
CRITICAL THEORY Stephen Eric Bronner
THE CRUSADES Christopher Tyerman
CRYPTOGRAPHY Fred Piper and Sean Murphy
THE CULTURAL REVOLUTION Richard Curt Kraus
DADA AND SURREALISM David Hopkins
DARWIN Jonathan Howard
THE DEAD SEA SCROLLS Timothy Lim
DEMOCRACY Bernard Crick
DERRIDA Simon Glendinning
DESCARTES Tom Sorell
DESERTS Nick Middleton
DESIGN John Heskett
DEVELOPMENTAL BIOLOGY Lewis Wolpert
THE DEVIL Darren Oldridge
DICTIONARIES Lynda Mugglestone
DINOSAURS David Norman
DIPLOMACY Joseph M. Siracusa
DOCUMENTARY FILM Patricia Aufderheide
DREAMING J. Allan Hobson
DRUGS Leslie Iversen
DRUIDS Barry Cunliffe
EARLY MUSIC Thomas Forrest Kelly
THE EARTH Martin Redfern

ECONOMICS Partha Dasgupta
EDUCATION Gary Thomas
EGYPTIAN MYTH Geraldine Pinch
EIGHTEENTH-CENTURY BRITAIN Paul Langford
THE ELEMENTS Philip Ball
EMOTION Dylan Evans
EMPIRE Stephen Howe
ENGELS Terrell Carver
ENGINEERING David Blockley
ENGLISH LITERATURE Jonathan Bate
ENVIRONMENTAL ECONOMICS Stephen Smith
EPIDEMIOLOGY Rodolfo Saracci
ETHICS Simon Blackburn
THE EUROPEAN UNION John Pinder and Simon Usherwood
EVOLUTION Brian and Deborah Charlesworth
EXISTENTIALISM Thomas Flynn
FASCISM Kevin Passmore
FASHION Rebecca Arnold
FEMINISM Margaret Walters
FILM Michael Wood
FILM MUSIC Kathryn Kalinak
THE FIRST WORLD WAR Michael Howard
FOLK MUSIC Mark Slobin
FORENSIC PSYCHOLOGY David Canter
FORENSIC SCIENCE Jim Fraser
FOSSILS Keith Thomson
FOUCAULT Gary Gutting
FREE SPEECH Nigel Warburton
FREE WILL Thomas Pink
FRENCH LITERATURE John D. Lyons
THE FRENCH REVOLUTION William Doyle
FREUD Anthony Storr
FUNDAMENTALISM Malise Ruthven
GALAXIES John Gribbin
GALILEO Stillman Drake
GAME THEORY Ken Binmore
GANDHI Bhikhu Parekh
GENIUS Andrew Robinson
GEOGRAPHY John Matthews and David Herbert
GEOPOLITICS Klaus Dodds
GERMAN LITERATURE Nicholas Boyle
GERMAN PHILOSOPHY Andrew Bowie
GLOBAL CATASTROPHES Bill McGuire
GLOBAL ECONOMIC HISTORY Robert C. Allen

GLOBAL WARMING Mark Maslin
GLOBALIZATION Manfred Steger
THE GOTHIC Nick Groom
GOVERNANCE Mark Bevir
THE GREAT DEPRESSION AND THE
  NEW DEAL Eric Rauchway
HABERMAS James Gordon Finlayson
HEGEL Peter Singer
HEIDEGGER Michael Inwood
HERODOTUS Jennifer T. Roberts
HIEROGLYPHS Penelope Wilson
HINDUISM Kim Knott
HISTORY John H. Arnold
THE HISTORY OF ASTRONOMY
  Michael Hoskin
THE HISTORY OF LIFE
  Michael Benton
THE HISTORY OF MATHEMATICS
  Jacqueline Stedall
THE HISTORY OF MEDICINE
  William Bynum
THE HISTORY OF TIME
  Leofranc Holford-Strevens
HIV/AIDS Alan Whiteside
HOBBES Richard Tuck
HUMAN EVOLUTION Bernard Wood
HUMAN RIGHTS Andrew Clapham
HUMANISM Stephen Law
HUME A. J. Ayer
IDEOLOGY Michael Freeden
INDIAN PHILOSOPHY Sue Hamilton
INFORMATION Luciano Floridi
INNOVATION Mark Dodgson and
  David Gann
INTELLIGENCE Ian J. Deary
INTERNATIONAL MIGRATION
  Khalid Koser
INTERNATIONAL RELATIONS
  Paul Wilkinson
ISLAM Malise Ruthven
ISLAMIC HISTORY Adam Silverstein
ITALIAN LITERATURE
  Peter Hainsworth and David Robey
JESUS Richard Bauckham
JOURNALISM Ian Hargreaves
JUDAISM Norman Solomon
JUNG Anthony Stevens
KABBALAH Joseph Dan
KAFKA Ritchie Robertson
KANT Roger Scruton
KEYNES Robert Skidelsky
KIERKEGAARD Patrick Gardiner
THE KORAN Michael Cook

LANDSCAPES AND
  GEOMORPHOLOGY
  Andrew Goudie and Heather Viles
LANGUAGES Stephen R. Anderson
LATE ANTIQUITY Gillian Clark
LAW Raymond Wacks
THE LAWS OF THERMODYNAMICS
  Peter Atkins
LEADERSHIP Keith Grint
LINCOLN Allen C. Guelzo
LINGUISTICS Peter Matthews
LITERARY THEORY Jonathan Culler
LOCKE John Dunn
LOGIC Graham Priest
MACHIAVELLI Quentin Skinner
MADNESS Andrew Scull
MAGIC Owen Davies
MAGNA CARTA Nicholas Vincent
MAGNETISM Stephen Blundell
MAO Delia Davin
THE MARQUIS DE SADE John Phillips
MARTIN LUTHER Scott H. Hendrix
MARTYRDOM Jolyon Mitchell
MARX Peter Singer
MATHEMATICS Timothy Gowers
THE MEANING OF LIFE
  Terry Eagleton
MEDICAL ETHICS Tony Hope
MEDICAL LAW Charles Foster
MEDIEVAL BRITAIN John Gillingham
  and Ralph A. Griffiths
MEMORY Jonathan K. Foster
METAPHYSICS Stephen Mumford
MICHAEL FARADAY
  Frank A. J. L. James
MODERN ART David Cottington
MODERN CHINA Rana Mitter
MODERN FRANCE
  Vanessa R. Schwartz
MODERN IRELAND Senia Pašeta
MODERN JAPAN Christopher
  Goto-Jones
MODERN LATIN AMERICAN
  LITERATURE
  Roberto González Echevarría
MODERNISM Christopher Butler
MOLECULES Philip Ball
THE MONGOLS Morris Rossabi
MORMONISM
  Richard Lyman Bushman
MUHAMMAD Jonathan A. C. Brown
MULTICULTURALISM Ali Rattansi
MUSIC Nicholas Cook

MYTH Robert A. Segal
THE NAPOLEONIC WARS
    Mike Rapport
NATIONALISM Steven Grosby
NELSON MANDELA Elleke Boehmer
NEOLIBERALISM Manfred Steger and
    Ravi Roy
NETWORKS Guido Caldarelli and
    Michele Catanzaro
THE NEW TESTAMENT
    Luke Timothy Johnson
THE NEW TESTAMENT AS
    LITERATURE Kyle Keefer
NEWTON Robert Iliffe
NIETZSCHE Michael Tanner
NINETEENTH-CENTURY
    BRITAIN Christopher Harvie and
    H. C. G. Matthew
THE NORMAN CONQUEST
    George Garnett
NORTH AMERICAN
    INDIANS Theda Perdue and
    Michael D. Green
NORTHERN IRELAND
    Marc Mulholland
NOTHING Frank Close
NUCLEAR POWER Maxwell Irvine
NUCLEAR WEAPONS
    Joseph M. Siracusa
NUMBERS Peter M. Higgins
OBJECTIVITY Stephen Gaukroger
THE OLD TESTAMENT
    Michael D. Coogan
THE ORCHESTRA D. Kern Holoman
ORGANIZATIONS Mary Jo Hatch
PAGANISM Owen Davies
PARTICLE PHYSICS Frank Close
PAUL E. P. Sanders
PENTECOSTALISM William K. Kay
THE PERIODIC TABLE Eric R. Scerri
PHILOSOPHY Edward Craig
PHILOSOPHY OF LAW
    Raymond Wacks
PHILOSOPHY OF SCIENCE
    Samir Okasha
PHOTOGRAPHY Steve Edwards
PLAGUE Paul Slack
PLANETS David A. Rothery
PLANTS Timothy Walker
PLATO Julia Annas
POLITICAL PHILOSOPHY David Miller
POLITICS Kenneth Minogue
POSTCOLONIALISM Robert Young
POSTMODERNISM
    Christopher Butler
POSTSTRUCTURALISM
    Catherine Belsey
PREHISTORY Chris Gosden
PRESOCRATIC PHILOSOPHY
    Catherine Osborne
PRIVACY Raymond Wacks
PROBABILITY John Haigh
PROGRESSIVISM Walter Nugent
PROTESTANTISM Mark A. Noll
PSYCHIATRY Tom Burns
PSYCHOLOGY Gillian Butler and
    Freda McManus
PURITANISM Francis J. Bremer
THE QUAKERS Pink Dandelion
QUANTUM THEORY
    John Polkinghorne
RACISM Ali Rattansi
RADIOACTIVITY Claudio Tuniz
RASTAFARI Ennis B. Edmonds
THE REAGAN REVOLUTION Gil Troy
REALITY Jan Westerhoff
THE REFORMATION Peter Marshall
RELATIVITY Russell Stannard
RELIGION IN AMERICA Timothy Beal
THE RENAISSANCE Jerry Brotton
RENAISSANCE ART
    Geraldine A. Johnson
RHETORIC Richard Toye
RISK Baruch Fischhoff and John Kadvany
RIVERS Nick Middleton
ROBOTICS Alan Winfield
ROMAN BRITAIN Peter Salway
THE ROMAN EMPIRE
    Christopher Kelly
THE ROMAN REPUBLIC
    David M. Gwynn
ROMANTICISM Michael Ferber
ROUSSEAU Robert Wokler
RUSSELL A. C. Grayling
RUSSIAN HISTORY Geoffrey Hosking
RUSSIAN LITERATURE Catriona Kelly
THE RUSSIAN REVOLUTION
    S. A. Smith
SCHIZOPHRENIA Chris Frith and
    Eve Johnstone
SCHOPENHAUER Christopher Janaway
SCIENCE AND RELIGION
    Thomas Dixon
SCIENCE FICTION David Seed
THE SCIENTIFIC REVOLUTION
    Lawrence M. Principe

SCOTLAND Rab Houston
SEXUALITY Véronique Mottier
SHAKESPEARE Germaine Greer
SIKHISM Eleanor Nesbitt
SLEEP Steven W. Lockley and
    Russell G. Foster
SOCIAL AND CULTURAL
    ANTHROPOLOGY
    John Monaghan and Peter Just
SOCIALISM Michael Newman
SOCIOLOGY Steve Bruce
SOCRATES C. C. W. Taylor
THE SOVIET UNION Stephen Lovell
THE SPANISH CIVIL WAR
    Helen Graham
SPANISH LITERATURE Jo Labanyi
SPINOZA Roger Scruton
SPIRITUALITY Philip Sheldrake
STARS Andrew King
STATISTICS David J. Hand
STEM CELLS Jonathan Slack
STUART BRITAIN John Morrill
SUPERCONDUCTIVITY
    Stephen Blundell
TERRORISM Charles Townshend
THEOLOGY David F. Ford

THOMAS AQUINAS
    Fergus Kerr
THOUGHT Tim Bayne
TOCQUEVILLE Harvey C. Mansfield
TRAGEDY Adrian Poole
TRUST Katherine Hawley
THE TUDORS John Guy
TWENTIETH-CENTURY
    BRITAIN Kenneth O. Morgan
THE UNITED NATIONS
    Jussi M. Hanhimäki
THE U.S. CONGRESS
    Donald A. Ritchie
THE U.S. SUPREME COURT
    Linda Greenhouse
UTOPIANISM Lyman Tower Sargent
THE VIKINGS Julian Richards
VIRUSES Dorothy H. Crawford
WITCHCRAFT Malcolm Gaskill
WITTGENSTEIN A. C. Grayling
WORK Stephen Fineman
WORLD MUSIC Philip Bohlman
THE WORLD TRADE
    ORGANIZATION Amrita Narlikar
WRITING AND SCRIPT
    Andrew Robinson

Available soon:

THE BRITISH CONSTITUTION
    Martin Loughlin
THE BRITISH EMPIRE Ashley Jackson

SYMMETRY Ian Stewart
HAPPINESS Dan Haybron
BACTERIA Sebastian G. B. Amyes

For more information visit our website
www.oup.com/vsi

Delia Davin

MAO

A Very Short Introduction

Great Clarendon Street, Oxford, OX2 6DP,
United Kingdom

Oxford University Press is a department of the University of Oxford.
It furthers the University's objective of excellence in research, scholarship,
and education by publishing worldwide. Oxford is a registered trade mark of
Oxford University Press in the UK and in certain other countries

© Delia Davin 2013

The moral rights of the author have been asserted

First Edition published in 2013

Impression: 1

All rights reserved. No part of this publication may be reproduced, stored in
a retrieval system, or transmitted, in any form or by any means, without the
prior permission in writing of Oxford University Press, or as expressly permitted
by law, by licence or under terms agreed with the appropriate reprographics
rights organization. Enquiries concerning reproduction outside the scope of the
above should be sent to the Rights Department, Oxford University Press, at the
address above

You must not circulate this work in any other form
and you must impose this same condition on any acquirer

British Library Cataloguing in Publication Data

Data available

ISBN 978–0–19–958866–4

Printed in Great Britain by
Ashford Colour Press Ltd, Gosport, Hampshire

Contents

Acknowledgements xi

Pronunciation and abbreviations xiii

List of illustrations xv

Map xvii

1 Becoming a revolutionary 1

2 Organizing revolution 15

3 Yan'an 31

4 First years of the People's Republic 48

5 The Great Leap Forward and its aftershocks 66

6 The Cultural Revolution: it's right to rebel 79

7 Decline and death 97

8 Legacies and assessments: the posthumous Mao 111

Timeline 125

References 129

Further reading 135

Index 139

Acknowledgements

I had the good fortune to live in Beijing between 1963–5 and 1975–6. The experience gave me an abiding interest in this period of Chinese history and I will always be grateful to the friends, students, and colleagues, many alas now dead, who showed me something of what life was like for Chinese then.

All scholars build on the work of their predecessors. In writing this short introduction to Mao, I have been able to consult the work of experts too numerous to list. I must, however, thank the late Stuart Schram by name. The doyen of Mao scholars in the West for over half a century, through his work he inspired and influenced all subsequent studies while his scholarly edited volumes of Mao's writing in translation provide invaluable source materials.

Thanks are due to the anonymous reader of my manuscript who made some very useful suggestions, to Owen Wells who read and commented on my first draft, and to the kind and competent staff of the NHS who kept me funtioning during the writing of this book.

Pronunciation and abbreviations

This book uses the hanyü pinyin system of romanization of standard Chinese. The transliterations that cause most problems for speakers of English are:

c   approximate pronunciation 'ts'

x   approximate pronunciation 'sh'

q   approximate pronunciation 'ch'

And the sounds chi, zhi, ri, si, shi, and zi are pronounced as if the 'i' sound is an r—chr, zhr, and so forth.

Abbreviations used in text and references

CCP   Chinese Communist Party
PLA   People's Liberation Army
SW   *Selected Works*

List of illustrations

1 Mao Zedong (right) aged 25 with his mother shortly before her death and his two younger brothers **13**
David King Collection

2 Yang Kaihui with her two elder sons, Mao Anying and Mao Anqing, 1924 **18**
David King Collection

3 Mao Zedong and He Zizhen in Yan'an, 1937 **41**
David King Collection

4 Jiang Qing (Lan Ping)—a Shanghai starlet in the 1930s before she met Mao **42**
David King Collection

5 Mao Zedong and Jiang Qing in Yan'an, 1937 **44**
David King Collection

6 Mao and Zhou Enlai, 1937 **45**
David King Collection

7 Mao, his nephew Mao Yuanxin, and his daughters Li Min and Li Na, 1951 **53**
From Philip Short, *Mao: A Life*, Hodder & Stoughton, 1999, supplied by David King Collection

8 Mao and his son Mao Anying, 1949 **54**
David King Collection

9 Cultural Revolution poster—Chairman Mao is the Red Sun in our Hearts **87**
David King Collection

10 Wang Guangmei, wife of Liu Shaoqi, humiliated by Red Guards **89**
David King Collection

11 Jiang Qing Cultural Revolution poster with caption saying 'Learn from Jiang Qing, pay respects to Jiang Qing' **91**
Stefan Landsberger, International Institute of Social History (Amsterdam)

12 Jiang Qing, Mao Zedong, Lin Biao, and Zhou Enlai during the Cultural Revolution **94**
AFP/Getty Images

13 Mao shakes hands with President Nixon, 1976 **104**
David King Collection

14 Jiang Qing and Zhang Yufeng (Mao's secretary/mistress), both wearing dresses designed by Jiang Qing and holding hands for the camera **109**
David King Collection

15 The leadership line-up at Mao's funeral. In this official print, Jiang Qing, Zhang Chunqiao, Wang Hongwen, and Yao Wenyuan have been brushed out. However, no attempt is made to pretend they were not there. The gaps, of course, make it obvious and the characters of their names have been replaced with xxx or xx **112**
David King Collection

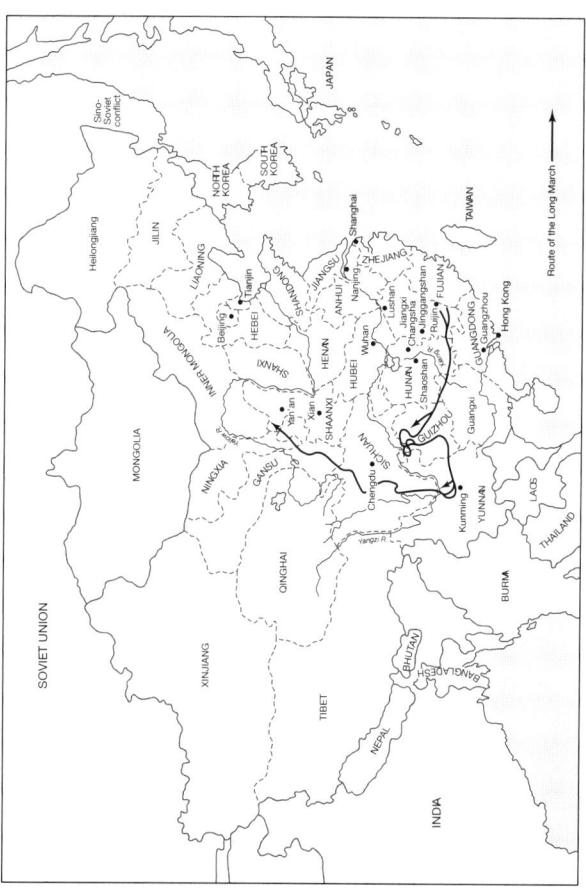

People's Republic of China under Mao

Chapter 1
Becoming a revolutionary

Mao Zedong is undisputedly the best-known Chinese of the twentieth century, an all-powerful leader and a major figure in modern world history. He was a revolutionary activist, organizer, and military commander for almost three decades before the communist victory, and he lived on for twenty-seven years shaping the history of the new People's Republic. Throughout his adult life Mao was a prolific writer. He produced a body of work on peasant revolution, guerrilla warfare, and class struggle in post-revolutionary society that influenced revolutionary movements both within China and in the rest of the world. The reception for his poetry and calligraphy was no doubt enhanced by his status as a leader, yet there is no denying his talent in these arts.

Under Mao's leadership China was transformed from a weak, disunited country to a power on the world stage. However, his vision for China's social transformation failed. He did not find a way to make China both egalitarian and prosperous and his efforts to do so visited enormous suffering on his people. During the Cultural Revolution his ruthlessness towards his opponents or those he perceived as opponents and his cynical exploitation of his cult of personality ultimately disillusioned many of his followers. By the time of his death, Mao's belief in constant class struggle and continuous revolution had become profoundly unattractive to ordinary people and the moral credibility of the Communist Party was ebbing away. His successors sought a new legitimacy for the communist-led state in the promise of improved standards of living. These were to be brought about through a return to a marketized economy, the abandonment of class struggle, and the acceptance of the development of considerable degrees of inequality. In sum, despite its extraordinary achievements, judged by Mao's own standards, his revolution was only a limited success.

At the time of Mao's birth in the last years of the 19th century, China was poor and weak. The Qing (Manchu) dynasty had been repeatedly discredited by its inability to defend the country against incursions on its sovereignty by Western and Japanese imperialism. In the period covered by this chapter, anti-imperialist nationalism developed as an important political force in China, informing the ideas of generations of young radicals. It found its strongest expression in the 1910s and 1920s in the iconoclastic May Fourth Movement whose thinkers stood for wholesale modernization and the rejection of China's Confucian past which they saw as backward-looking, patriarchal, and hierarchical. The Chinese Communist Party (CCP) of which Mao was a founder member and the Nationalist Party or Guomindang eventually became bitter enemies, but both grew out of this nationalism and both declared their determination to free China from imperialist domination and to build a strong modern state.

The dynasty was overthrown by the 1911 revolution, but the republic that replaced it proved a disappointment to revolutionary hopes. China suffered decades of political disunity, civil wars, and corrupt and ineffective governments. The limited economic progress that took place for a few years from 1928 under the Guomindang was quickly undone under the pressure of Japanese invasion and world war.

When the communist government took power in 1949, it united China under the strong government for which nationalists had yearned for so long. The remaining foreign interests in China were largely taken over by the state. By the time of Mao's death, largely due to the revolution that he led, the basis had been laid for large-scale industrialization and rapid economic growth. Living standards, health, and education had all made great progress. However, Mao's ruthlessness and vanity also brought catastrophe. Millions of Chinese suffered and died as a result of some of his disastrous mistakes.

Family

Mao's background was humble. He was born on 26 December 1893 to a rural family in Shaoshan village, Xiangtan county, in the southern province of Hunan. As a young man, Mao's father had bought a little land with money he had managed to save as a soldier. Through hard work and strict economy he gradually extended his holdings and employed a farm labourer. Later he also increased the household income by money lending and trading in grain. Ironically, had the household survived to experience the communist land reform, its members would have been classified as rich peasants or possibly even landlords, and suffered accordingly.

Most of what we know about Mao's childhood is derived from the account of his life that he gave in 1936 to the American journalist Edgar Snow, who later published it in his classic *Red Star over China*. Interestingly, although Snow recorded that Mao at first saw no point in recording his personal history, the account that he eventually gave is detailed, self-reflective, and clearly intended to show how his past had formed his beliefs and shaped his actions. It also prepared the ground for the myth of the infallible revolutionary leader.

Mao's mother bore seven children in all. Four died in infancy. The survivors were Mao himself and his two younger brothers, Mao Zemin, born 1896, and Mao Zetan, born 1905. There was also an adopted daughter, Zejian, the child of a paternal uncle. We may guess that Mao's influence on them was considerable as all three followed him into the communist movement. Zejian was executed in 1930, Zetan died in battle in 1935, and Zemin was killed by a warlord in 1943.

As a small child Mao lived for some years at the house of his maternal grandmother. When he returned to Shaoshan he often quarrelled with his father whom he recalled as mean, harsh, and demanding, yet the young Mao benefited from the comparative prosperity that his father had won for the family. He began to help on the land when he was 6 but was also fortunate enough to attend the village primary school and to go further afield for education in his teens. He had the privilege, unusual in a village family, of a room of his own where he could read until late in the night.

Mao's love of his mother was in sharp contrast to his hostility towards his father. A devout Buddhist, she sometimes incurred her husband's wrath by her generosity to the poor. Years later Mao claimed that the family had been divided into two camps; 'the Ruling Power', i.e. his father, and 'the Opposition', made up of Mao himself, his brothers, and sometimes even the hired labourer. However, Mao's mother was a peacemaker, whereas Mao could be confrontational. He recollected a quarrel in which he had cursed his father in front of many guests and stormed off, threatening to drown himself in a pond. His mother tried to persuade him to return but his father demanded an apology and a kowtow as a sign of submission. In the end, Mao agreed to give a one-kneed kowtow if his father would promise not to beat him. From this he claimed he had learnt that if he defended his rights by open rebellion his father would relent.

Mao's father, who had only had two years' schooling, took a utilitarian view of education. He wanted his eldest son to master the abacus and to be competent to take over the farm accounts. Later, when the family lost a lawsuit to an opponent who produced an apt quotation from the Chinese classics in court, he was forced to recognize the use of classical study.

The young Mao loved the great story cycles of Chinese literature, often based on the history of rebellions, such as *The Three Kingdoms*, *The Water Margin*, and *Journey to the West*. Written in the vernacular, such books were not part of the approved classical canon. Like countless other Chinese schoolboys Mao read them surreptitiously in class. But he also showed a gift for the classics and seems to have enjoyed them once he had got beyond the stage of rote learning. In later life, his speeches and his writings were full of allusions to the classics and to popular Chinese culture whereas he referred to Marxist classics rather sparingly.

By the time Mao was 13, there were six mouths to feed in the family. His father forced him to leave school to begin full-time work on the land. At 14 he was married to a cousin on his father's side, four years his senior. For his parents there was nothing extraordinary in such a match. Their own arranged marriage had taken place when his father was 15 and his mother 18. However, Mao told Edgar Snow that he never slept with this woman nor considered her his wife. She died in 1910, when he was 16. This experience no doubt contributed to the fierce opposition to arranged marriages expressed in his early writings.

In the same year, bored by farm work, Mao enrolled at a modern school 17 miles away in his mother's home district of Xiangxiang. Although Mao recalled that his father had opposed this move, he must in the end have agreed to finance it, perhaps because his next son, Zemin, three years Mao's junior, was now old enough to start working on the land. Mao, an outsider to the district, was teased about his shabby clothes by the better-off boys, but he made some friends at this new school and was liked by the teachers. Most importantly his intellectual horizons were expanded. He heard, belatedly, that the emperor and the empress dowager had died two years earlier in faraway Beijing and that Pu Yi, the new boy emperor, was on the throne. In addition to the traditional curriculum of the Chinese classics, this school offered 'western learning' including the natural sciences, English, music, world history. Mao read about figures as varied as Napoleon and Wellington, Peter the Great and the Empress Catherine, Gladstone, Rousseau, Montesquieu, Lincoln, and George Washington in books on 'great world heroes'. Through this filter Mao encountered for the first time the history of other nations, the ideas of the European Enlightenment, and the spirit of 19th-century nationalism. He also read about Kang Youwei and Liang Qichao, two classically trained scholars exiled for their advocacy of political reform in China, and under Kang's influence he became for a time a constitutional monarchist. One teacher at the new school had even studied in Japan. He had cut his queue (a long braid, the hairstyle imposed on Chinese men by the Manchu dynasty) when abroad and now had to wear an artificial one, which earned him the nickname of the 'false foreign devil'. Within a few years, the modernizing new Republic of China would forbid the wearing of the queue, but in 1910 the lack of one was interpreted as an act of defiance against the emperor and had to be concealed.

Leaving home

Soon Mao wanted more than Xiangxiang could offer. In 1911, aged 17, he journeyed the 40 miles to Changsha, the provincial capital, to enrol in another school. It was a time of great political ferment. In the first years of the 20th century the Qing dynasty had made some concessions to reform. These included attempts to create a modernized army with a trained officer core, a new government structure, the abolition of the traditional civil service examinations, the establishment of government schools teaching a modern curriculum, and, in 1908, the creation of elected assemblies intended to 'advise the government'. The dynasty hoped that limited change would stem the demand for more. Instead it whetted the appetite for reform. Moreover, army officers, teachers, and civil servants in the new institutions, as well as the students enrolled in modern schools, tended to favour reform or even revolution.

Changsha was a thriving river port connected to the coast by a tributary of the Yangzi River. When Mao arrived there, modernizing influences had only just begun to affect the city. Its gates still closed at dusk. There were as yet no cars, bicycles, or motor roads and ordinary people lived in a maze of narrow alleys and lanes without running water or sanitation. Hunan had had comparatively little direct experience of foreign incursion in the 19th century and its scholar gentry had been considered conservative Confucian revivalists. This had started to change in the last years of the 19th century as provincial officials and the scholar gentry together established new schools and libraries and began to encourage industry and commerce. The 1903 Treaty of Shanghai with Japan opened Changsha to foreign trade. Trade in Hunan's agricultural products grew as steamships took increasing quantities of rice, tea, tung oil, and timber down river. Foreign consuls built western-style houses on an island in the river with unheard-of luxuries including electric light. Missionaries arrived in the city. Modern schools and colleges flourished. Hunan became a centre of radicalism, and the patriotic railway rights movement which sought to recover the control and ownership of Chinese railways from foreign interests was particularly strong in the province.

Mao would have found Changsha an exciting place. Revolutionary and republican ideas were discussed in the radical press. Mao soon read his first newspaper and heard of the Tongmenghui, a revolutionary secret society led by Sun Yatsen that was opposed to the rule of the Manchu dynasty. He expressed his sympathy with the revolutionary ideas he encountered by cutting off his queue and forcing some of his friends to do likewise. As he admitted in his interview with Edgar Snow, he had come a long way since he had mocked the False Foreign Devil a year earlier.

On the outbreak of the 1911 revolution, Mao joined the army which was in revolt against the Qing dynasty. He gained little military experience; instead he spent his time drilling, cooking, and reading newspapers. He made friends with some ordinary soldiers and earned their gratitude by writing their letters for them. One thing showed how quickly he had absorbed traditional ideas of the scholar elite. Although he had so recently laboured in his father's fields, he now felt it would not befit his status as a student to carry his own water back to the barracks as his fellow soldiers did. Instead he used part of his meagre wage to purchase water from a pedlar. (When he came to power he would condemn such attitudes and ensure that students and white-collar workers all did regular stints of manual labour.) Mao decided to leave the army and resume his studies after six months. By then, the emperor had abdicated and a militarist leader, Yuan Shikai, had been installed in Beijing as the first president of the new republic.

Intellectual influences

In his search for a future Mao drifted in and out of schools for soap making, police training, law, and commerce, apparently easily swayed by advertisements or the recommendations of friends. His longest stay was six months at the First Provincial Middle School where he did some serious study of traditional Chinese ideas of governance. He then dropped out of school altogether in favour of an intensive programme of reading in the provincial library. Here, for the first time, he saw a map of the world. His reading included Rousseau's *Social Contract* and Montesquieu's *The Spirit of Laws*, which introduced him to Enlightenment ideas of the freedom of the individual, equality, and the compact between the ruler and the ruled. Other works he recalled were Adam Smith's *Wealth of Nations*, Darwin's *Origin of the Species*, 'a book on ethics by John Stuart Mill', and 'Herbert Spencer's *Logic*'. There is some confusion of some titles here, but the selection is not an improbable one. Rousseau, Montesquieu, and Darwin had been translated from Japanese (accessible to more Chinese scholars than European languages) around the turn of the century. In the same period, Yan Fu, a scholar who had studied in England in the 1870s, published Chinese translations of Thomas Huxley, Adam Smith, and Hebert Spencer. Yan Fu believed that in order to achieve wealth and power, China needed not only technological expertise, but also political and social reform and an understanding of western social sciences. These texts caused enormous excitement in China. Both reformers and revolutionaries seized on the concepts of natural selection and the survival of the fittest to argue that unless China modernized it was doomed to weakness and defeat. Such ideas formed an important backdrop to Mao's political development.

Mao was forced to abandon his self-study because his father refused to support him any more unless he enrolled at a school. He then decided to become a teacher and in 1913 he entered the Hunan Teachers' College from which he graduated in 1918. He was clearly not a particularly easy student. He was threatened with expulsion for taking part in a student protest against the school management. On another occasion he grabbed the collar of a teacher with whom he was arguing. He refused to work at the natural sciences because he did not like them. He also objected to a compulsory course in still life drawing. For the still life exam he drew a simple oval that he entitled 'Egg'. Fortunately his high marks in social science compensated for his poor performance in these other subjects.

Despite such incidents, Mao's time at the Hunan Teachers' College was important to his intellectual development. The courses were systematic and challenging. He was later to remember two of his teachers with particular respect. Yuan Zhongqian, nicknamed Yuan the Big Beard, forced him to improve his classical Chinese style. Yang Changji, the head of the philosophy department, a veteran of ten years' study in Aberdeen, Berlin, and Tokyo, made the deepest impression. Mao spoke of him as an idealist who urged his students to try to be useful to society.

On Yang Changji's recommendation, Mao read a Chinese translation of *A System of Ethics* by the neo-Kantian philosopher Friedrich Paulsen. This inspired Mao to write an essay, for which he received a mark of 100. The essay no longer exists but Mao's copy of the book does. His marginal notes amount to more than 12,000 Chinese characters (equivalent to around 8,000 English words), showing how seriously he took it. Mao made many comparisons between western and Chinese thought, seeing both similarities and differences. Paulsen's discussion of the nature of man, and of altruism and egotism, drew his attention. He was also interested in Paulsen's assertions about the relationship between the free will, the influence of the society, and moulding or self-cultivation. Mao's notes reflect his lasting preoccupation with change:

> It is the times when things are constantly changing and numerous men of talent are emerging, that people like to read about. When they come to periods of peace, they are bored and put the book aside. It is not that we like chaos, but simply that the reign of peace cannot last long, is unendurable to human beings, and that human nature is delighted by sudden change.

Steeped in Confucian discipline, Mao, like his teachers, was attracted by Paulsen's idea of self-cultivation through self-discipline. He had already applied these ideas to his own life, studying hard, dressing simply, and exercising regularly. In the summer of 1916 he and a classmate had even tramped through the countryside living on what villagers would give them in order to see if they could manage without money. Decades later, the idea that hardship and austere living were good for the character, and for the development of 'political consciousness', was discernible in the way people were exhorted to live in revolutionary China.

It was Yang Changji who introduced Mao to *New Youth*, which from 1915 to 1926 was a major national forum for discussions on the transformation of society. In 1917 the journal carried Mao's first published article. In it he emphasized the relationship of physical education to the health and strength of both the individual and the state, and attributed China's weakness to the disparagement of physical attainments in traditional culture. These were not particularly original ideas in radical circles at the time, but publication in *New Youth* was a significant achievement for a young man from an inland province. The article also reflected Mao's preoccupation with the cultivation of a strong will without which, he said, nothing could be achieved.

Mao began to realize the value of organizations in his student years. In 1917, he was a founder member of the New People's Study Society, a student discussion group. Several of its members later joined the Communist Party. In 1918, when Mao graduated, he went to Beijing where his former teacher, Yang Changji, had been appointed professor of ethics. Yang introduced Mao to Li Dazhao who was the librarian at the Beijing University and a co-editor with Chen Duxiu of *New Youth*. Li found him a job as a library clerk. With a post at China's leading university, associating with the most brilliant radical scholars, and in love with Yang Changji's daughter, Yang Kaihui, Mao seemed to have found the life he wanted. But all was not what it seemed and he was disappointed. His stipend was tiny, his living conditions miserable, and worst of all, when he tried to engage the famous radicals he so admired in conversation on political and cultural subjects, the busy men had no time for an assistant librarian speaking a southern dialect. There has been speculation that Mao's later harshness towards intellectuals may have been due to his resentment of this treatment.

After a winter in Beijing, Mao accompanied some of his Hunan friends to Shanghai. They were on their way to a work-study programme in France. Mao claimed that he had decided not to go with them because he thought he should learn more about his own country. His lack of funds and the knowledge that he was a poor linguist may also have influenced his decision to return to Changsha.

Soon after Mao left the capital it was convulsed by the May Fourth demonstration, a furious response to the news of the republican government's acceptance of the Treaty of Versailles that provided the post-First World War settlement. China had declared war on Germany in 1917 and had sent labour battalions to Europe to assist the British and the French behind the lines. At the end of the war China expected that as one of the allies it would recover rights over Chinese territory previously ceded to Germany. Instead, under the Versailles Treaty, these interests were to pass to Japan. The protest demonstration in Beijing began a wave of protest that engulfed the country. The modernizing movement that had been under way since 1917 henceforth became known as the May Fourth Movement. Its demands included not only the rejection of the Treaty, but also the adoption of science and democracy as guiding principles for government, the replacement of classical Chinese in favour of the vernacular written language in order to facilitate mass literacy, and changes in the family and the position of women. For intellectuals of Mao's generation the May Fourth Movement was the formative experience.

Back in Changsha, Mao found that his brothers had brought his mother to the city for medical treatment (see Figure 1). When she died in October, Mao wrote a touching eulogy for her. His father's death from typhoid a few months later predictably affected him less. Meanwhile, he threw himself into political activities. He wrote articles and took on the editorship of two student papers that were later suppressed by the provincial government. In November, Changsha was disturbed by the suicide of a young woman called Miss Zhao who had cut her throat behind the curtains of the sedan chair in which she was being carried to a wedding forced on her by her parents. The tragedy inspired Mao

1. Mao Zedong (right) aged 25 with his mother shortly before her death and his two younger brothers

to write nine articles attacking the evils of arranged marriage. At this time educated women were still a tiny minority. Some women took part in the May Fourth Movement, but much of the writing advocating women's emancipation was produced by men, many of whom, like Mao, had developed an interest in what was called 'the Woman Question' because of their own experience of arranged marriage.

Mao became involved in Hunanese provincial politics and a movement for Hunanese self-government at this stage. He returned to Beijing at the beginning of 1920 on a mission to campaign against the governor of Hunan. While he was there, Professor Yang Changji died. This event brought Yang Kaihui and Mao closer, but she soon left with her mother to accompany her father's coffin to Changsha. In Beijing, Mao was able to read some works about Marxism and became enormously excited by *The Communist Manifesto*, newly translated into Chinese. In April, back in Shanghai, he briefly earned a living as a laundryman and again met Chen Duxiu, the editor of *New Youth*. Chen had earlier been imprisoned in Beijing for distributing inflammatory literature. On release he took refuge in the French concession in Shanghai where he organized a small Marxist group. By July, Mao judged it safe to return to Changsha and he became involved in another Marxist study group. He also joined one that studied the Russian revolution. In September he was appointed head teacher of a primary school, a post that he held for two years. Financially secure at last, he married Yang Kaihui. At this stage, despite his interest in Marxism, Mao was uncertain of his beliefs and was attracted by anarchist ideas of mutual aid and shared resources. Only in January 1921, in a letter to his friend Cai Hesen, who was studying in France, did Mao finally repudiate anarchist ideas and accept Marx's materialist conception of history. He had found the ideology on which he would base the rest of his life.

Chapter 2
Organizing revolution

After the establishment of the Republic of China in 1912, no single national government achieved control over the whole of China. Shifting alliances of warlords, each with their own power base, controlled the national government at Beijing. Many provinces functioned as semi-independent entities ruled by local warlords. Rivalries were fought out in numerous civil wars. The main power base of the revolutionary groups and secret societies that had overthrown the Manchu dynasty was in the south. In 1917, their leader, Sun Yatsen, set up a government in the southern city of Guangzhou and in 1919 he reorganized these revolutionary groups as the Guomindang or Nationalist Party.

In the summer of 1921, delegates from various small provincial communist groups came to the First Congress of the Chinese Communist Party (CCP). Representatives of the Comintern sent to China from Moscow were in attendance. Immediately, the tensions that would characterize Sino-Soviet relations for years to come began to appear. First, Moscow was trying to assert leadership over the international communist movement through the Comintern. The Chinese communists resented the Comintern's assumption of supremacy. Secondly, Moscow, and therefore the Comintern, was ambivalent about the potential of communist movements in underdeveloped countries. Orthodox Marxism had created the expectation that revolutions led by communist parties and based on the industrial working class would first occur in capitalist countries. When the October 1917 revolution in Russia was not followed by successful revolutions in industrialized Western Europe, Moscow was isolated. By 1924, Stalin was arguing that 'socialism in one country' was possible. Soviet Russia sought to break its isolation by supporting anti-imperialist or anti-colonialist movements in colonized countries. According to the Marxist analysis of history, these still agrarian societies might be ready for bourgeois democratic revolutions but not socialist ones, for these required a working class. The Comintern line was therefore that communist parties in 'backward' countries could survive only by cooperating closely with nationalist movements. The CCP however required its members to break all ties with all other political organizations. The Comintern representatives viewed this as an error and urged the tiny Chinese Party to ally itself with the Guomindang.

Mao as a teacher

Mao, who attended the Congress as a Hunan delegate, spoke only briefly and was not elected to the Central Executive Committee of the CCP. As yet a little known figure in the communist movement, he would have appeared very provincial in Shanghai, in his traditional long cotton gown and cloth shoes. When he returned to Hunan, he obtained provincial government backing to set up a 'Self-study University' at which students would 'read on their own and study together'. Its constitution contained ideas on education that Mao would promote at other times in his life, notably during the Cultural Revolution. For example, the university was to be inclusive, admitting students without formal qualifications if they were capable of benefiting from the courses. It would bring together the intellectual class and working class and have a horticultural garden, a print shop, and ironworks, putting an end to the Chinese tradition that intellectuals did not engage in physical labour or sports. Despite a focus on modern thought and Marxism, the curriculum also gave space to traditional Chinese learning, reflecting Mao's belief that Chinese should not neglect their own history and culture.

Although Mao headed this school, most of his time from 1921 to 1923 was devoted to political activity and labour organization. He was the branch secretary of the Hunan branch of the CCP formed in October 1921. Less than a year later it had thirty members, a size equalled only by branches in Shanghai and Guangzhou. Mao also worked with the labour organizations that were appearing in Hunan in the coal, zinc, and lead mines and among railway workers and employees in the electrical, textile, and garment industries. He was joined in this by his two brothers, his wife, pregnant with their first child, and friends from the New People's Study Society recently returned from France. Although there were successful strikes in Hunan, urban workers were still a tiny minority in China and their organizations weak. In February 1923 a massacre of forty striking railway workers in north China carried out by a warlord highlighted the vulnerability of the labour movement and strengthened the argument that it needed nationalist allies.

The United Front

By 1923, the Comintern had pushed the CCP into agreeing to a united front with the Guomindang. In Guangzhou, Sun Yatsen accepted Russian advisers to help him reorganize his party. In accordance with the new Party policy, Mao became a Guomindang member. In 1923 he was elected to the CCP's Central Executive Committee at the Party's Third Congress in Guangzhou. At the Congress, he spoke of the revolutionary potential of the peasant movement. He pointed out that peasants were far more numerous in China than workers, and had been the main force in numerous past rebellions. After some time in Shanghai, in September Mao returned to Changsha where a new civil war threatened. He left again in January 1924, just after the birth of his second son, to attend the First National Congress of the Guomindang in Guangzhou. Yang Kaihui was distressed at being left alone with two young children. Mao reacted by writing a poem that expressed his feelings of desolation that they were parting on bad terms.

Having been elected an alternate member of the Guomindang's Central Executive Committee at the Congress, Mao went to do United Front work in Shanghai where Yang Kaihui and the children joined him in the summer (see Figure 2). By the end of

2. **Yang Kaihui with her two elder sons, Mao Anying and Mao Anqing, 1924**

1924 he was back in Changsha on sick leave. He then retreated to his home village with his wife and children and spent some months in the Hunan countryside investigating peasant conditions.

Soon he moved from investigating to organizing peasant associations. The May 30th Incident of 1925, in which Chinese demonstrating against the mistreatment of workers by foreign factory owners were shot by British-officered police in the International Concession of Shanghai, triggered a wave of nationalist outrage all over China and massive increases in membership for both the Guomindang and the CCP. In Hunan, the incident stimulated peasant militancy. Mao's belief in the revolutionary potential of the peasants was reinforced. When he returned to Guangzhou in October, he was made acting head of the Guomindang Propaganda Department, a post he occupied for eight months, and his expertise on the peasantry was recognized by his appointment as principal of the Guomindang Peasant Training Institute.

This was a time of great tension in Guangzhou, the seat of the Guomindang government. Sun Yatsen's death from cancer the previous March had been followed by a struggle for succession between the right and left wing of the Guomindang. In March 1926 Chiang Kaishek made a bid for the Party leadership by declaring martial law, arresting a number of CCP members, and putting his Russian advisers under house arrest. The affair was smoothed over when the Russians agreed to a military expedition to the north to achieve national reunification under a Guomindang government. Chiang Kaishek was confirmed as the Guomindang leader. When new restrictions on CCP members holding office in the Guomindang were introduced, Mao lost his position in the Propaganda Bureau but continued to work for the Peasant Training Institute.

Peasant revolution

Mao was not the only communist leader to insist on the revolutionary potential of the peasants but it was a point of difference between him and most of the CCP leadership. The peasant question was complicated. The Comintern advisers of course took the orthodox Marxist line that the proletariat or industrial working class must be the leading class in a *socialist* revolution, but they nonetheless urged the CCP to get involved in the agrarian revolution, insisting that in agrarian countries without a sizeable working class, a successful *nationalist* revolution directed against imperialist domination required the support of the peasants. Comintern advisers were frustrated with the CCP leadership for ignoring the peasantry, yet they criticized Mao for overestimating the revolutionary nature of the peasants and even alleged that his analysis seemed to give peasants the role of the proletariat. Some CCP leaders regarded the peasants as backward, ignorant, and irrelevant to the modern revolutionary society they wished to build. As a party, the Guomindang formulated a policy towards the peasants, and set up training institutes for them earlier than the CCP. However, many Guomindang officials, like many in the CCP leadership, were ambivalent about the peasant movement as violence against landlords increased and condemned it as 'out of control'.

One of Mao's most dynamic pieces of writing is his 'Report on the Peasant Movement in Hunan', of February 1927. This report was the result of another visit to Xiangtan and Xiangxiang where the vigour of the peasant movement led him to argue that the countryside was the key to successful revolution in China. He challenged revolutionaries to support the peasant movement:

> In a very short time in China's central, southern and northern provinces, several hundred million peasants will rise like a mighty storm, like a hurricane, a force so swift and violent that no power, however great, will be able to hold it back. They will break through the trammels that bind them and rush forward along the road to liberation. They will send all imperialists, warlords, corrupt officials, local bullies and evil gentry to their graves. All revolutionary parties and all revolutionary comrades will stand before them to be tested, to be accepted or rejected by them. To

march at their head and lead them? To trail behind them, gesticulating and criticising them? To face them as opponents? Every Chinese is free to choose among the three, but the circumstances demand that a quick choice be made.

Rebuking those who feared the violence of the peasant movement and thought that it was going too far he wrote:

> A revolution is not a dinner party, or writing an essay, or painting a picture, or doing embroidery; it cannot be so refined, so leisurely and gentle, so temperate, kind, courteous, restrained, and magnanimous. A revolution is an insurrection, an act of violence by which one class overthrows the power of another.

Almost four decades later, this passage would be included in the 'Little Red Book' and studied by the whole Chinese population during the Cultural Revolution. The memorable phrase 'A revolution is not a dinner party' was frequently quoted by Red Guards to justify their own violent actions.

The report also reflected Mao's concern for the position of women. He observed that like men in rural Chinese society, women suffered under three forms of authority—political, clan, and religious—but they also had to endure a fourth, the authority of men.

Neither the 'Hunan Peasant Report', nor the analysis of classes in rural China that Mao had written in 1926, read much like orthodox Marxism. He appears to negate the orthodox Marxist view that the working class must be the leading class in the revolution by asserting:

> To give credit where credit is due, if we allot ten points to the accomplishments of the democratic revolution, then the achievements of the city dwellers and the military rate only three points, while the remaining seven points should go to the peasants in their rural revolution.

This passage was dropped when Mao's *Report* was tidied up for his official *Selected Works* published in the 1950s, as was his advocacy of sexual freedom. But the main importance of the *Report* was that it presented the peasantry as a class capable of playing a leading role in the revolution, a vision that was fundamental to Mao's ideas and strategies.

The end of the United Front

The political situation in China was increasingly turbulent. The Northern Expedition was launched in the summer of 1926 to bring warlord-controlled north China under the control of the Guomindang. A left-leaning Guomindang government was set up in the important central China city of Wuhan, while Chiang Kaishek established his headquarters at Nanchang and prepared an advance on Shanghai. Chinese businessmen and foreigners in the city who saw Chiang as a dangerous radical were at first very alarmed. The labour movement welcomed him. Shanghai's General Labour Union called for a strike and an armed insurrection against the warlords and in support of the Nationalist army. However, Chiang had decided to break with the left which he saw as threatening his leadership of the Guomindang. When his Nationalist troops entered the city at the end of March, Chiang was quick to win the support of industrialists, bankers, and secret society bosses and to reassure the foreigners that their interests were safe. On 12 April he began a vicious campaign of suppression against the labour movement. Many activists were shot and hundreds more arrested.

The repression destroyed much of the CCP organization in Shanghai. The Comintern's insistence on preserving the United Front with the Guomindang at all costs left the CCP ill prepared for Chiang's switch of allegiance. Forced underground in Shanghai, the CCP fell back on an alliance with the left Guomindang government at Wuhan. But even this was uneasy and in any case the Wuhan government soon collapsed. The

Comintern advisers fled back to the Soviet Union, and Guomindang generals began the suppression of peasant associations in Hunan and Hubei. Chiang Kaishek assumed total control over the Guomintang and set up a new government of the Chinese Republic based in Nanjing.

The veteran Marxist intellectual Chen Duxiu was blamed for these reverses. He was accused of opportunism and betrayal, and dismissed as secretary general of the CCP. His replacement was the Russian-trained Qu Qiubai. In a desperate attempt to retrieve the situation, the CCP organized a series of abortive urban insurrections, the Nanchang Uprising in early August, the Autumn Harvest Uprising led by Mao in September, and the Guangzhou (Canton) Commune in December. This last took place under direct orders from Moscow where Stalin wanted a victory for his policies in China to strengthen him in his battle against Trotsky. It ended in rapid defeat and the brutal slaughter of anyone identified as a radical. By the end of 1927, the communist movement in China was at its lowest ebb. It had suffered heavy casualities, and its organization in the cities had gone underground.

The establishment of rural base areas

In October, Mao, who had led a small peasant army in the Autumn Harvest Uprising, fled with his remaining troops, about 1,000 in all, into Jinggangshan, a mountainous area straddling the Hunan–Jiangxi border. In the course of the next year he joined forces with two other communist commanders, Zhu De and Peng Dehuai, who were similarly taking refuge with the rump of their troops. Together they developed the Chinese Red Army. In the recriminations that followed the defeats, Mao was censured by the Party Centre for recklessness and deprived of his alternate membership of the Central Committee. Mao did not learn of his disgrace for some months. The lesson he drew from the disasters of 1927 was that, as he wrote, 'political power is obtained from the barrel of a gun'. Ten years later, in 1938, he would expand the idea,

> Every Communist must grasp the truth, 'Political power grows out of the barrel of a gun.' Our principle is that the Party commands the gun, and the gun must never be allowed to command the Party. Yet, having guns, we can create Party organizations...We can also create cadres, create schools, create culture, create mass movements. Everything in Yan'an has been created by having guns. All things grow out of the barrel of a gun. According to the Marxist theory of the state, the army is the chief component of state power.

On both occasions, Mao was explaining his strategy of using military power to build rural bases, preferably on remote provincial borders where Nationalist or warlord control was weak. In these 'base areas' or border regions, also called soviets, communist local governments could be protected by communist armies. However, Jinggangshan was not a successful base. Mao was later to comment that it was exceedingly difficult for Bolshevism to take root there. The communist policy of land distribution met with resistance even from poor peasants who identified with their lineage rather than with other poor peasants, and the area was too impoverished to provide a good base for expansion. At the start of 1929, Mao and Zhu De moved their troops south to Ruijin, a small town on the borders of Jiangxi and Fujian. Here they developed a communist base, later grandiloquently called the Jiangxi Soviet Republic, which the Red Army held until 1934.

In Ruijin, as later in the communist base areas in the north, the CCP leadership had a social laboratory in which policies could be tried out. Land was redistributed. Zhu De and Mao recognized that the behaviour of the Red Army was key to mustering local support. They worked out training programmes designed to instil discipline and self-respect in soldiers who had been recruited in part from bandits and vagrants. New marriage regulations gave women equal rights, outlawed arranged marriage, and made divorce available at the request of either partner. Efforts were made to involve women in political activities and in support work for the army.

Mao's relations with the Party Centre remained difficult. At the CCP's Sixth Congress held in Moscow in 1928, he was elected to the Central Committee but not to the Politburo. The man who emerged as the real leader, Li Lisan, was a Hunanese, known to Mao since their student days in Changsha. Li had been a labour organizer and believed in urban revolution. He was critical of what he called Mao's failure to recognize the petty-bourgeois nature of the peasantry. He now began to urge Mao and Zhu De to disperse their forces and to mobilize peasants over a much wider area. Mao was even ordered to leave the army and go to Shanghai to receive orders.

Mao, able to prevaricate over this order partly because communications with the Party Centre were so poor, remained in Jiangxi trying to consolidate his base. He argued that because China was a semi-colonial country in which the imperialist powers could be played off against one another, and because it was made up of many localized agricultural economies, it was possible for 'red power' to exist in scattered bases if the army was sufficiently strong. This would be his strategy for the next twenty years.

Personal life

At this juncture Mao's personal life was also fraught. He had lost contact with Yang Kaihui in October 1927, soon after she had given birth to their third son. In 1928, in Jinggangshan, he began to live with He Zizhen, an 18-year-old teacher who bore six children in the nine years of their union. While she was pregnant with her first daughter she took part in gruelling marches and guerrilla warfare. The child was born in autumn 1929 when Mao was recuperating from malaria in Fujian province. Perhaps troubled at the situation, Mao wrote to Li Lisan asking him to obtain a postal address for Yang Kaihui from his brother Mao Zemin, who was in Shanghai. Yang Kaihui, meanwhile, was still with her three sons in Changsha. She wrote letters and poems to Mao that were never sent but were discovered years later, in the

1980s, hidden in the wall of her old house. These indicate that she knew of his infidelity and was profoundly distressed.

When Mao and He Zizhen left Fujian to return to a life of forced marches and fighting, they left their daughter with a peasant family for safety. It has been rumoured that her maternal uncle traced her in the 1970s but she never met Mao or her mother again. He Zizhen's second child, a boy called Maomao, was born in 1932. In 1934 a third son died soon after birth.

Military and political ideas

In the Jiangxi period, despite constant movement and involvement in political and military affairs Mao still found time to write. In January 1930, in a letter to a fellow revolutionary, Lin Biao, he again put forward the case for building up red political power in small base areas where land reform could be carried out and the communist military forces gradually built up. They would then be in a strong position to take advantage of a revolutionary high tide when it came. Mao opposed this to Lin's strategy of simply engaging in mobile guerrilla warfare in the hope that the masses would be won over and at some future point there would be a national insurrection. He accused both Lin and the Central Committee of pessimism in their assessments. This document was originally published under the title 'Letter to Comrade Lin Biao'. However, when an edition of Mao's *Selected Works* was under preparation in 1948, Lin objected to the critical references to him being given publicity. They were duly withdrawn and the piece appeared as 'A Single Spark can Start a Prairie Fire'. When the references to Lin were restored in the 1991 edition, the 'Single Spark' title was preserved.

By 1930, the strength of the Red Army in the Jiangxi Soviet had reached 60,000–70,000. These numbers allowed Li Lisan to propose a new policy of attacks on the cities. Mao was at first reluctant, but in the end seems to have participated enthusiastically.

He and Zhu De attacked Nanchang that summer, while Peng Dehuai took Changsha but held it only for a few days. Ultimately, the policy proved a disaster and the communist armies retreated to their base areas. In Changsha, Mao's wife Yang Kaihui was among the civilians executed. She refused to save her life by denouncing her husband. Her sister-in-law took the children to Shanghai to be cared for by the Party. The youngest boy became ill and died. When the Party organization collapsed the older two had to live on the streets for several years. Later, the Party found them again and they were sent to the Soviet Union. Mao did not forget Yang Kaihui. Almost thirty years after her death he commemorated her loyalty and heroism in a poem 'I have lost my proud poplar'.

The disastrous failure of the CCP attacks on the cities was blamed on Li Lisan. He was recalled to Moscow and the CCP leadership in Shanghai passed to a group who had studied in Moscow. In the base areas Mao attempted to assert his leadership in the course of the Futian incident, which involved a vicious purge of communist activists and soldiers loyal to Mao's rivals. The details of this disturbing incident in late 1930 still remain obscure; Mao claimed that the 2,000–3,000 men killed had been members of the 'Anti-Bolshevik League' but in fact it seems to have been a factional struggle within the communist movement.

Mao conducted surveys of the social and economic life of villages within the Jiangxi Soviet in 1930 and used his findings for the formulation of land and family policies. He was named Chairman of the Provisional Central Government at the First All-China Congress of Soviets in Ruijin in November 1931. However, his status and roles diminished in the next three years. Moscow had accepted the central importance of the Chinese soviet areas and the Red Army and Russian-returned students were becoming more prominent in their leadership. Meanwhile, the existence of the CCP in the cities was becoming ever more difficult. Ironically, when the CCP leadership was forced to relocate to Ruijin from

Shanghai in January 1933, its belated recognition of the rural revolution put Mao under increasing pressure. The CCP leadership disputed his military strategy of drawing enemy forces deep into soviet territory before engaging them. He was also criticized for the moderation of his land policies. Until the evacuation of Jiangxi in 1934, Mao was sometimes busy with practical or administrative work, but at other times he lived in seclusion, struggling with malaria and tuberculosis. It seems he was also angry at his political exclusion.

The Long March

The Jiangxi Soviet was under pressure from Guomindang armies for the whole of its existence. Even the occupation of China's north-eastern provinces by the Japanese in 1931 did not reduce Chiang Kaishek's determination to eliminate the communists. He used encirclement strategies with military and economic blockades to try to make life in the soviet areas impossible. By autumn 1934, the Guomindang's fifth encirclement campaign had become so effective that the decision was taken to evacuate the soviet areas. This was the beginning of what became known as the Long March. Of 100,000 people who left Jiangxi, 85,000 were soldiers. Only 35 were women, mainly the wives of communist leaders. Other family members, the sick, and the wounded were left behind. Some activists also stayed to defend the rear, among them Mao's brother Mao Zetan. Mao's pregnant wife, He Zizhen, was allowed to leave with the Long March, but it was out of the question to carry children on the difficult retreat. She entrusted her son Maomao to her sister He Yi who had married Mao Zetan. The boy was hidden by his uncle with a peasant family. Unfortunately, Mao Zetan was then killed and no one knew where Maomao was. He Yi returned to search for him after 1949 but her efforts were unsuccessful.

The Long March arrived in the communist base area of northern Shaanxi almost a year after it had left Jiangxi. After the revolution, the Long March was made part of the mythology of the Chinese Revolution and celebrated in stories, songs, and films as a great triumph. At its start, however, it was a retreat with no clear objective. The communist forces covered about 8,000 miles over some of China's most difficult terrain, often forced by the movements of the enemy to change their plans. The March involved great heroism but also the grim reality of exhaustion, starvation, and death. There were casualties in constant skirmishes. Many dropped out or died of disease or exhaustion. Only one in ten reached the north. Mao's wife He Zizhen gave birth to a fourth child, who had to be abandoned with peasants. Two months later, she suffered serious shrapnel wounds but survived.

Mao's political standing rose during the Long March. In January 1935, at Zunyi in Guizhou province he was named as a full member of the Politburo and chief military adviser to Zhou Enlai, previously one of his critics. The Zunyi meeting also passed some critical resolutions that reflected Mao's views on the errors of military strategy in the last years in Jiangxi. The meeting was not, as it was subsequently presented in CCP mythology, the moment at which Mao triumphed; however, it can be seen as the first step in his rise to the leadership of the CCP. He would still have to struggle with rivals for several more years, but he was increasing his following among the Red Army officers who regarded him as the most successful of their leaders.

Under attack from Guomindang troops and local warlords, the Long March moved westward into Yunnan from Guizhou and then turned north through Sichuan and eastern Tibet. Many men were lost to the struggle with hunger, exhaustion, and frostbite. Mao himself was sick with malaria and had to be carried on a stretcher. In northern Sichuan the Long Marchers met up with a much larger communist group from a soviet in eastern Sichuan, led by Zhang Guotao, another founder member of the CCP. Zhang wanted to build a new base area on the Sichuan border but Mao contended that they should push further north to establish a base from which they could organize resistance to the Japanese. For a time the communist forces split. Zhang Guotao and Zhu De remained in Sichuan until they suffered severe defeats and were forced north with a much reduced force to join Mao. Meanwhile, Mao's group struggled on across the mountains and through the dangerous swamplands in some of the most remote areas of China until it reached northern Shaanxi in October 1935. Here Mao would spend the next decade developing the political organization, popular support, and military power that would eventually allow him to take power in the whole of the Chinese mainland.

Chapter 3
Yan'an

The region in which the Red Army now settled was poorer and more backward than the communist border regions in the south. Its yellow, crumbly loess soil gives the eroded hills their strange colour. When the wind blows across the arid land it deposits a thin layer of dust on everything. Water is precious and has to be conserved for agriculture by painstaking terracing. Caves are cut into the hillsides to form dwellings that are warm in winter and cool in summer, leaving the ground above free for cultivation. The staple food is millet, a grain the newly arrived southerners found hard to tolerate.

From January 1937 the capital of the Shaanxi-Gansu Soviet (later the Shaan-Gan-Ning Border Region) was Yan'an, a remote county town deep in the hills. For the next ten years, the name Yan'an came to stand for the Chinese communist movement. In the first months after his arrival in Shaanxi, Mao was frequently on the move, active in manoeuvres, battles, and recruitment carried out to renew the Red Army and expand the new base. Subsequently, however, he made his home in a two-roomed cave in Yan'an with He Zizhen and their fifth child, a girl, Li Min, born after the Long March. Here he began a more settled life than he had known for many years.

Relations with the Guomindang

From the time of its arrival in the north-west, the CCP positioned itself as anxious to build a broad national alliance to fight Japanese imperialism, although not necessarily including the Guomindang Party leader Chiang Kaishek. After the occupation of China's three north-eastern provinces, Chiang had played a waiting game in relation to the Japanese, trying to postpone war but at the same time preparing for it. In addition to building up the military, part of this preparation was to try to unify China under Guomindang rule and eliminate the communists. He famously remarked that the Japanese were a disease of the skin, while the communists were a disease of the heart. In public documents, the communists often referred to Chiang as a Japanese lackey, yet they put out feelers for negotiations. When, in summer 1936, the CCP established radio contact with Moscow for the first time in two years, Stalin, whose primary concern in international policy was now the threat posed by fascism, urged stronger efforts to conciliate Chiang Kaishek. For his part Mao sent Moscow urgent appeals for material support. This eventually reached Yan'an in December in the form of a cash payment sent through sympathizers in Shanghai.

At the end of 1936 a dramatic incident convulsed China. Xi'an, the provincial capital of Shaanxi, was garrisoned by troops from north-east China under Marshal Zhang Xueliang. Though nominally under Guomindang command, these troops and their commander were not enthusiastic about the policy of eliminating the communists before resisting the Japanese; after all, their homeland was under Japanese occupation. On 12 December Zhang Xueliang arrested Chiang, who had flown into Xi'an to urge joint action against the communists. Zhang then informed Mao and Zhou Enlai that he would not release Chiang until the Guomindang agreed to create a coalition government.

The communist leaders were ecstatic at the misfortune that had befallen their old enemy and there is evidence that at first they considered trying to have Chiang executed. Eventually, however, they used the situation to push for a united front. After negotiations involving Zhou Enlai, Zhang Xueliang, and Chiang's wife and brother-in-law who flew in from Nanjing, Chiang was released. Although he made no public undertaking, it was implied that he would end the civil war. Thus, to the relief of the Russians who still saw Chiang as potentially the most effective national leader against the Japanese, the Xi'an Incident ended peacefully. It is now thought that the logic of events would soon have forced Chiang into an alliance with the CCP, even without the Xi'an Incident. In July 1937, the Japanese launched new hostilities against the Guomindang. A declaration of war followed and the anti-Japanese coalition between the Guomindang and the CCP became a reality.

The war with Japan

Early in the war most of coastal China was lost to the Japanese with heavy casualties. The Guomindang capital, Nanjing, was sacked with extreme brutality in December 1937. The new capital, Wuhan, inland on the Yangzi River, fell to the Japanese the following October and the Guomindang moved further up the Yangzi to Chongqing far in the west of China. The Japanese set up puppet regimes in north and central China. Communist units engaged in bitter fighting in various parts of China and organized underground resistance and guerrilla warfare in areas under enemy control, but Yan'an itself was remote from most of the conflict.

In Jiangxi, Mao had been directly involved with fighting and therefore was constantly on the move. In Yan'an, although preoccupied with Party, administrative, and military affairs, he had more time to read and think. He acquired a young secretary,

Chen Boda, who had studied in Moscow and could help him to draft his essays. He read translations of Marxist works and prepared a lengthy series of lectures on Marxism-Leninism for delivery in 1937 at Yan'an's Resistance University. The lectures later became the basis for his first lengthy theoretical works, 'On Practice' and 'On Contradiction'. Formerly, his writing had mostly consisted of reports, resolutions, military orders, letters, and surveys directly relevant to immediate problems. These new essays staked his claim to be acknowledged not only as a successful military and political leader, but also as a Marxist theoretician. Even in these theoretical pieces, however, Mao insists on the primacy of experience over book-learning, advancing one of his basic positions that 'All genuine knowledge originates in experience' and that one must 'discover truth through practice and through practice again verify the truth'. The two essays became required reading for communist cadres in Yan'an. Decades later, after Mao's death, these ideas would be used by Deng Xiaoping to attack the habit of using Mao's works as scripture in situations to which they were not relevant.

Struggling for the Party leadership

Mao had begun his progress towards supremacy in the Party leadership at Zunyi. He continued the struggle in the north-west. By the end of the Long March he had accumulated a considerable reputation for making the right administrative and military decisions. Many of his earlier rivals had been discredited by mistakes that had led to setbacks for the communist movement. The most serious threat to his leadership in the Yan'an was from Wang Ming, one of the 'returned Russian students' through whom Stalin tried to exert his authority over the CCP back in 1929. Wang Ming arrived in Yan'an at the end of November 1937 after six years in the Soviet Union. Like Stalin, Wang favoured closer cooperation with Chiang Kaishek on terms which Mao feared would mean the loss of the CCP's independence. Wang quickly began to assert his authority, using his prestige as both a

Marxist theorist and a Comintern office holder. With characteristic exaggeration, Mao later complained that after Wang Ming's return 'my authority did not extend beyond my cave'. Although in autumn 1937 Moscow seemed to recognize Mao's de facto leadership over the CCP, Wang Ming's return to China and his subsequent appointment to head the CCP's United Front Office in Wuhan posed a challenge to Mao. Wang's policies of close cooperation with the Guomindang had considerable support from the Politburo, including Zhou Enlai.

Mao's rivalry with Wang Ming and his determination to assert his authority is reflected in his writings in these years. In 'Problems of Strategy in the Anti-Japanese Guerrilla War' and 'On Protracted War' published in 1938 he set out his views on military strategy, clearly opposing Wang as he explained why China could win the war, why it would be protracted, and why guerrilla tactics should be used in it. In November, in 'The Question of Independence and Autonomy within the United Front and Problems of War and Strategy' he explained his views on the nature and limitations of cooperation with the Guomindang, insisting on the need to retain military capacity under the control of the CCP and repeating his famous aphorism 'Political power grows out of the barrel of a gun'.

In 1940 Mao published 'On New Democracy', an essay carefully framed to rally support from a non-communist audience. It presented the CCP as a party to be supported by all sincere nationalists, the rightful heir to the May Fourth Movement and a force that would govern in the interests of the people as a whole and would rid China of foreign imperialism.

Meanwhile, Wang Ming's position was fatally compromised by the course of events. First, the Guomindang's prestige suffered as it conceded one city after another to the Japanese, culminating in the loss of Wuhan in late October 1938. Wang was forced to return to Yan'an, thus losing his independent base. Later, the United

Front itself was threatened. Alarmed by the CCP's military successes and the expansion of its base areas, Chiang Kaishek imposed a blockade of the Shaan-Gan-Ning base. More dramatically, at the beginning of 1941, the communist New Fourth Army in east central China was ambushed by a superior Guomindang force resulting in the loss of 9,000 men. The New Fourth massacre discredited Mao's rivals and boosted his reputation. His insistence that the CCP must preserve its independent military strength within the United Front now appeared prescient. Despite all this, the United Front survived in name at least. Both sides needed it. Soon the entry into the war of the Soviet Union in June 1941, and the United States in December, put both the Guomindang and the CCP under greater pressure from international sponsors determined that they should cooperate.

Problems in the communist areas

In north China the communists had held territory with a population of 45 million people. Japanese successes reduced this to territory with only 25 million. Their indiscriminate terror tactics against the civilian population in the villages created support for the CCP which in the long run built an underground resistance capable of waging guerrilla war. However, the immediate situation for the communists was grim. Their territory had shrunk, it was isolated by the Guomindang blockade, they lacked military supplies, and the poverty of their territory made it difficulty to feed and support the army and the communist bureaucracy.

Mao's response was to try to increase production and to cut government expenditure. Village enterprises using indigenous technology made goods that could no longer be imported from outside. Peasant cooperatives were encouraged. The army and the bureaucracy were cut and everyone was urged to grow their own vegetables. Solders were taught to spin. Recent research has also shown that the export of opium grown in the base area was quietly permitted to flourish. The border regions survived and even grew. By 1945 their population had reached nearly 100 million. Mao's policies after 1949 often reflected nostalgia for the successful mass mobilization policies of this era.

Rectification and Mao's authority

In this period Mao used the Rectification Movement 1941–4 to consolidate his power within the Party. This movement in which all Party member and cadres eventually had to participate was a programme of intensive study, reflection, criticism, and self-criticism that prefigured political practice after the establishment of the People's Republic. Study materials included 'On New Democracy' and various other documents that set out Mao's view of Party history exposing the errors of his former opponents and rivals in the leadership. A core document was Mao's essay 'Reform our Study' in which he attacked what he called subjectivism, sectarianism, and dogmatism and accused some Party members of 'studying the theories of Marx, Engels, Lenin and Stalin in the abstract, without any aim, and without considering their relevance to the Chinese revolution'. Another lively essay argues in Mao's earthy style that shit is more useful than dogma: 'A dog's shit can fertilise the fields and a man's can feed the dog. And dogmas? They can neither fertilise the field nor feed the dog. Of what use are they?' (References to shit were later expurgated in the version that appeared in the official *Selected Works*.) The campaign quickly gained the support of most of the leadership and was extended to the rank and file of the Party. Everyone had to study the rectification documents, absorb Mao's view of Party history, and consider their own past roles. Even such a senior figure as Zhou Enlai, henceforth Mao's loyal lieutenant, made an abject self-criticism for his past opposition.

The Rectification Campaign established Mao's works as a canon in which the correct application of Marxism-Leninism to

Chinese realities could be found and therefore the source of correct thought and action for Chinese communists. Even the creative arts came under new Maoist guidelines contained in a course of lectures Mao gave in 1942, later published as the 'Yan'an Talks on Art and Literature'. These basically demanded that art and literature should serve the revolution and that political criteria should be put ahead of artistic ones in judging the quality of creative works. Until the death of Mao in 1976, the 'Talks' were used to impose an increasingly repressive literary orthodoxy.

Three of Mao's essays from the Yan'an period were used for decades for political education at a more popular level. 'In Memory of Norman Bethune' (1939) paid tribute to the revolutionary internationalism of a Canadian doctor who had died caring for the wounded of the communist Eighth Route Army. In 'Serve the People' (1944), commemorating the death of an ordinary communist soldier, Mao quoted the Han dynasty historian Sima Qian (c.145–87 BC) saying that though 'death befalls all men alike, it may be weightier than Mount Tai or lighter than a feather'. To die serving the people was of course weightier than Mount Tai. Finally, 'The Foolish Old Man who Moved the Mountains' (1945) recounted the story of an old man who did just that. When mocked for his foolishness in attempting this hopeless task he argued that if he did not achieve it his sons or their sons would. The analogy was drawn with the victory that would one day be won in China by the CCP.

For many Chinese intellectuals, Yan'an under Mao came to symbolize a modest utopia. They saw it as a revolutionary society free from corruption and from the restrictions the traditional family imposed on the individual, offering effective opposition to the Japanese and hope for a new China. Patriots made their way to it from both Guomindang China and the Japanese-occupied areas. Their hopes were not wholly delusory but Yan'an certainly had its dark side. Rectification was hard on its victims. When the well-known writer Ding Ling had arrived in Yan'an from Shanghai in 1936, Mao sent her a poem praising her decision to join the revolution:

> Yesterday a young lady of literature
> Today you have become a general.

This did not save her when she published a critique of the way women were treated in Yan'an on 8 March (Women's Day) 1942. She was dismissed as editor of the *Liberation Daily* and sent to labour in the countryside. Wang Shiwei, another young communist writer from Shanghai who published a critique of the increasingly hierarchical nature of Yan'an society, suffered a more terrible fate. He was put before mass criticism meetings, accused of Trotskyism, imprisoned for several years, and, in what Mao was later to say had been a mistaken action, summarily executed in 1947. These were well-publicized cases. The many other mass criticisms, detentions, and expulsions made people increasingly cautious about expressing opinions.

In 1943, Mao finally attained supreme leadership of the CCP, being elected chairman of the Politburo and of the Central Committee. In April 1945, the seventh Party Congress, the first to be held since 1928, confirmed his appointments. All members of the new Politburo were Mao's associates. Mao could now afford to show some generosity to his opponents—Wang Ming and two of his faction were included in the Central Committee—but Congress records reflect Mao's control. *The Resolution on Party History* passed at the Congress reviewed the vicissitudes of revolutionary struggle since 1921, criticizing a long list of Mao's opponents for their 'left and right errors' and asserting that after the Zunyi Conference the Party had gained strength and rigour from correct leadership of comrade Mao Zedong. In one of many paeans of praise to Mao's correct leadership, Liu Shaoqi called him both China's greatest revolutionary and statesman and greatest theoretician and scientist. The new Party constitution presented by Liu to the Congress asserted that the CCP was guided in all its work by Mao Zedong Thought. This was defined as the doctrine that integrates the theories of Marxism-Leninism with the practice of the Chinese Revolution. The basis for the cult of Mao's personality was thus established.

Enter Jiang Qing

Mao's private life underwent difficult changes in the Yan'an years (see Figures 3 and 4). From his observations in 1936, Edgar Snow thought that Mao and He Zizhen were seen as an ideal couple; in fact, there were problems. He Zizhen became pregnant yet again in 1937. She wanted to go to a good hospital in Shanghai for an abortion and to get the shrapnel removed from her wounds. When the Japanese occupation of the city made this plan impossible, she decided to go to the Soviet Union instead. Influenced by her belief that Mao was having an affair, she seems to have decided to break with him permanently. Her sixth and last child, born in Moscow in 1938, survived only a few months. Mao then sent their 2-year-old daughter Li Min to live with her. Mao's two sons by Yang Kaihui, who had been rescued from a life scavenging on the streets of Shanghai, were already at school in Russia. For a time He Zizhen lived with all three children. Later, she was diagnosed as mentally ill and stayed in a Soviet clinic before returning to China in 1947. After the communist victory, she was awarded a pension but not the post to which her revolutionary past should have entitled her. Only after Mao's death did she come back into the public eye as a member of the People's Consultative Congress in 1979. Her memoirs were published and, when she died in 1984, the old Party leaders honoured her and her ashes were placed with those of other revolutionaries in Babaoshan in Beijing. The eulogistic accounts of her life that appeared after her death implied a favourable contrast with Mao's fourth wife Jiang Qing who had by then been imprisoned by the post-Mao leadership.

3. Mao Zedong and He Zizhen in Yan'an, 1937

Soon after He Zizhen's departure, Mao started to live with a pretty young woman originally from Shandong who had been a struggling actress in Shanghai under the stage name Lan Ping—Blue Apple (see Figure 4). Mao gave her the name Jiang Qing. Lan Ping had leftist connections and decided to try her luck

4. Jiang Qing (Lan Ping)—a Shanghai starlet in the 1930s before she met Mao

in Yan'an where she was able to use an old friendship with a fellow provincial, the Politburo member Kang Sheng, to become a drama instructor at the Lu Xun Academy. As the CCP's security expert, Kang had been involved in purges of the Party both in China and in Moscow, where he lived from 1933 until he returned to China in 1937 with Wang Ming. Although he had worked closely with Wang, Kang soon switched his allegiance to Mao and supervised intelligence operations not only against the Japanese and the Guomindang, but also against opponents of Mao within the Party.

Kang was soon able to do Mao a personal favour. Mao's new liaison gave rise to unease in the top echelons of the Party. Jiang Qing seemed an unworthy replacement for He Zizhen whose heroic sufferings during the Long March were remembered. Other women veterans were particularly disapproving of the liaisons formed by male leaders with attractive young women arriving from the cities. Rumours about Jiang Qing's past, both personal and political, led to questions about her suitability as a wife for Mao. Kang Sheng, who insisted that she was a Party member in good standing, gave her security clearance. This no doubt strengthened his relationship with Mao. Mao then defiantly insisted that he had the right to decide on his own marriage (see Figure 5). However, probably as a result of the disapproval of old comrades, Mao kept his new wife largely in the background running his household and his office. She did not play a prominent role until the Cultural Revolution when Mao needed people whose loyalty he could count on. The couple had one daughter, Li Na, born in 1940.

Photographs from Yan'an show Mao as a striking, commanding figure. He was tall for a Chinese, gaunt from the privations of the Long March, with thick black hair worn unusually long. On his chin was a prominent black mole, considered a sign of good fortune in China. Some of his personal habits were and would remain less compelling. He disliked baths, preferring to be wiped down with hot towels. He smoked heavily and spat and hawked regularly to relieve his bronchitis. He believed that drinking tea was the most effective way to clean teeth and so never used a toothbrush. He slept badly and was addicted to sleeping pills. These were perhaps a cause of the constipation about which he frequently complained to members of his household. He was still fit, however, and would soon need to be. The end of the war

5. Mao Zedong and Jiang Qing in Yan'an, 1937

6. Mao and Zhou Enlai, 1937

with Japan would bring an end to his settled life in the Yan'an cave he shared with Jiang Qing (see Figure 6).

Civil War and the establishment of the People's Republic

When Japan surrendered in 1945, a few months of negotiations between the Guomindang and the CCP followed. In reality both sides were preparing for civil war but neither wished to appear to initiate it. Both were sensitive to the public's longing for peace; moreover, their patrons in Washington and Moscow favoured coalition government. The CCP no doubt resented the Soviet position. Mao had become aware that at Yalta, and again at Potsdam, Stalin had received assurances that the Chinese Eastern Railroad and Lüshunkou (Port Arthur), former imperial Russian concessions in China that had been ceded to Japan in 1905, would be returned to the Soviet Union. Stalin had also assured Roosevelt and Churchill that the Guomindang was the only party capable of ruling China after the war and he signed a treaty with Chiang in 1945 acknowledging him as the leader of China's legal government. In exchange Chiang recognized the independence of Outer Mongolia, and agreed to the continued Soviet occupation of Lüshunkou and control of the Chinese Eastern Railway. Meanwhile, despite outside pressure, negotiations between the CCP and the Guomindang soon broke down and civil war ensued.

In the civil war the CCP initially seemed disadvantaged in terms of territory, arms, and military might, but the Guomindang was disunited, inept, and corrupt. Despite large amounts of American aid, it lost the advantage as inflation and financial scandal made it increasingly unpopular and sapped the will of its troops to fight. The communists by contrast had high morale and tight organization. Above all, they had the support of China's peasant majority, for the peasants stood to gain from the radical land redistribution that the communists now offered. Many urbanites thought of the CCP only that that it could hardly be worse than the Guomindang, but as the communists began to take the towns, they gained a reputation as incorruptible and efficient.

Mao took overall command of the communist armies and switched from guerrilla tactics to a large-scale but highly mobile warfare in which 'luring enemy forces in deep' and then surrounding and isolating them was important. Having initially given ground and even evacuated Yan'an, from 1947 the renamed People's Liberation Army (PLA) gained territory. In January 1949 it took Beijing, in April it crossed the Yangzi, defying Stalin's advice that the CCP should settle for a communist government in the north and a Guomindang one in the south. By the end of the year the Guomindang government had fled to Taiwan and the CCP controlled the Chinese mainland.

On 1 October 1949 Mao Zedong, with his characteristic talent for symbolic gestures, stood on the rostrum of the old Forbidden City overlooking Tiananmen to proclaim the birth of the People's

Republic. His declaration, 'the Chinese people have stood up', was calculated to appeal to nationalism. His decisive control over his Party had involved freeing it from Soviet domination and he was now able to promise a New China that would be free from all foreign interference. It was a promise that had great appeal to his fellow countrymen.

Yan'an

Chapter 4
First years of the People's Republic

Mao now became Chairman of the People's Republic while remaining Party Chairman. As he held leading positions in both the Party and the state, his story after 1949 is inseparable not only from the struggles within the Party that had dominated his life for so long but also from China's political, social, and economic development. Mao's very strong ideas on policy were also constantly evolving. He had considerable constitutional power but it was not absolute. In the first years of the People's Republic the collective leadership of the Party was responsible for policy, and policy decisions and disagreements were debated by the Politburo. Later, when Mao disagreed with his colleagues he showed an increasing tendency to use his prestige to ignore or crush opposition and act on his own authority. Mao influenced the development of all major policies in China until his death.

Now in his mid-fifties, Mao was no longer the gaunt young revolutionary whose informal manners and bright curiosity had impressed Edgar Snow in 1936. He had put on weight and his face had filled out. Access to him had become difficult even during the Yan'an days as the security around him became tighter. In Beijing he was an increasingly remote and almost mythical figure. With the other top Party and state leaders he took up residence in Zhongnanhai, part of the old complex of imperial palaces landscaped with lakes, trees, and pavilions. Like the others he was hidden behind its great red gates and high vermilion walls. When he left the complex he was whisked to appointments in large black Soviet-made sedans hung with lace curtains that concealed the identity of the occupants. He travelled around China in a private train. He had always liked to rise late and read far into the night and to see people by sending for them at short notice. In his later years he would summon colleagues, journalists, and even foreign statesmen late in the evening or after they had gone to bed, a practice that emphasized his authority and put visitors at a psychological disadvantage.

The immediate policy directions of the new People's Republic were laid down in Mao's essay 'On the People's Democratic Dictatorship'. The leadership of the revolution was now in the 'hands of the proletariat', but it would rely on a bloc composed of the workers, peasants, the petty bourgeoisie, and the national bourgeoisie. He explained that for the moment the CCP would regulate capitalism, not destroy it. In the testing times ahead, he acknowledged that the CCP would need the help of professional people: '…we have won the basic victory in the revolutionary war.… But…our past work is only the first step in a long march.… We shall soon put aside some of the things we know well and be compelled to do things we don't know well.… We must learn to do economic work from all who know how, no matter who they are. We must esteem them as teachers.' Such formulations allowed the CCP to attract support from business people, professionals, and intellectuals who were desperately needed to reconstruct the battered economy and to bring about the industrialization desired by the CCP. Although many educated Chinese fled to Hong Kong or Taiwan, the majority stayed on, hoping that the CCP would be able to fulfil its promise to rebuild China.

Relations with the Soviet Union

Mao also made it clear that China would seek an alliance with the Soviet Union. He knew that this policy of 'leaning to one side' would cause concern. Many educated Chinese greatly admired the United States, conscious of its wealth and power but also seeing it as the home of freedom and democracy. Many also felt negative about the USSR because the Soviet Red Army had pillaged north-east China of its industrial equipment when it liberated the territory from the Japanese at the end of the war. Ideologically and geo-politically, however, the policy of 'leaning to one side' was inevitable and was adopted after tentative and probably not very serious soundings about establishing relations with the USA had come to nothing.

Mao travelled by train to Moscow to see Stalin in December 1949. Unlike many other CCP leaders he had never been abroad. He spent three months in the Soviet capital. He was later to say of this stay that he had argued with Stalin for two months. It was doubtless a difficult time. Stalin wished to make clear his continuing authority as leader of the socialist camp. Mao was prepared to respect that position, but, formed by the nationalism of his generation, was sensitive to any suspicion that China was not being treated as an equal. Moreover, Mao was doubtless conscious that ill-judged orders from Moscow had cost the CCP dear in the past and had at one time threatened Mao's own place in the Chinese Party leadership.

Mao's resentment must have been increased by the terms of the Treaty of Friendship, Alliance, and Mutual Assistance that Moscow offered. Stalin exacted similar concessions on Lüshun and the Eastern Railway to those made by Chiang Kaishek in 1945 although the concessions were now time-limited. In an arrangement which for the Chinese was another echo of imperialism Stalin also insisted on the creation of Sino-Soviet joint stock companies for mineral exploitation in north-west

China. All too aware of the war-shattered state of the Soviet economy, he offered financial and technical aid in the form of credits that would later have to be repaid.

The Korean War

Soon the Korean War put new strains on the Sino-Soviet relationship. It began in June 1950 when the North Korean army, well armed by the Soviet Union, swept south through the divided peninsula. The UN Security Council immediately condemned North Korea as an aggressor. Troops under a UN flag, mainly from the United States, landed in the south and pushed north with a UN mandate to unite the country. Some Chinese leaders were reluctant to become embroiled in another war, but Mao feared that the USA might otherwise take the opportunity to attack the infant People's Republic, not least because China's main industries lay just north of the Yalu River that formed the Korean border. He also believed that participation would bring China prestige within the socialist camp and confer on the CCP the leading role in revolutionary Asia that the Soviet Party had in Eastern Europe.

Once the UN forces crossed the 38th parallel that had demarcated North and South Korea, Mao urged intervention, despite the anxiety of colleagues who felt that China was too weak for a direct confrontation with the United States. Although poorly armed, China's army of 1.2 million 'volunteers' was so numerous that it was able to push the UN forces back. Negotiations based on the division of Korea at the 38th Parallel began in July 1951 and an armistice was signed in 1953. Unbelievably, in this short war, the Chinese suffered almost one million casualties. Participation cost China dear in other ways. It confirmed the US adoption of Taiwan as a client state, isolated Beijing diplomatically, and increased its dependence on Moscow. Having been branded as an aggressor by the UN, the People's Republic was excluded from the UN until 1971. China's seat was instead occupied by the rump Guomindang government in Taiwan. China's expenditure on the war was US$10 billion. The Chinese were disappointed that the Soviet Union did not provide the air support they had expected and resentful at having to pay the USSR for military supplies when they felt they were fighting on behalf of the whole socialist camp.

Working from his headquarters in Zhongnanhai, Mao relinquished day-to-day control of the war to Peng Dehuai, the commander of the Chinese People's Volunteers in Korea, but exchanged frequent telegrams with him, keeping close control over strategy. Documents released by Beijing in the 1990s show that he also oversaw relations with the Soviet Union in minute detail while pushing his vision of socialist revolution and reconstruction in China.

At home in Zhongnanhai

Mao's household in this period was complicated. Jiang Qing, her daughter Li Na, and Li Min, Mao's daughter by He Zizhen, all lived with him in Zhongnanhai. Mao Anying and Mao Anqing, the sons of Yang Kaihui who had returned from the Soviet Union in 1946, and Mao Yuanxin, the son of Mao's brother Mao Zemin, who had been killed in 1941, were also part of this large household (see Figure 7).

Mao's feelings for his two sons were no doubt mixed with his feelings of guilt and nostalgia about their mother. After 1949 he arranged for them both to visit their mother's grave and to meet her mother in Changsha on the occasion of her birthday. Later he invited the nursemaid who worked for him and Yang Kaihui to visit him in the capital on several occasions. He sent regular remittances to his former mother-in-law, and was helpful to other members of Yang Kaihui's family. Mao received many requests for assistance from relatives on both his mother's and his father's sides and from former classmates and acquaintances. He normally resisted suggestions from supplicants that they should come to

7. Mao, his nephew Mao Yuanxin, and his daughters Li Min and Li Na, 1951

Beijing. He sent money to cases he thought deserving, always making clear that it came from personal funds, but he usually resisted suggestions that he should intervene with the authorities on their behalf, urging instead that they go through the proper channels.

The Korean War brought tragedy very close when Mao Anying was killed in November 1950 aged 28 (see Figure 8). It is said that Peng Dehuai and other leaders did not want Anying to risk his life in Korea, but Mao disagreed, asking, 'Who will go if my son doesn't?' Ironically this echoes his words to Anying a few years earlier when Anying wanted to marry a woman who was not yet 18, the minimum age at which women could marry under communist marriage law. 'Who will obey the regulations if my son does not?' he demanded. The couple married when she came of age in 1949 and Mao gave them a heavy winter coat that he said they could sleep under. When Mao heard of his son's death he said, 'It was his misfortune to be Mao Zedong's son.' Mao could not eat or sleep but sat smoking all day. He continued to treat Anying's young widow as a member of his family but urged her to remarry, which she eventually did.

8. Mao and his son Mao Anying, 1949

Mao's surviving son, Mao Anqing, worked as a translator when his health permitted, but was often in hospital with a mental illness, sometimes attributed to a beating he received from a policeman when he lived on the streets of Shanghai. Probably as a result of his disability, he did not marry until the age of 37, yet he lived to be 84. He had a son, born in 1970. His wife, the sister of his brother's widow, rose to be a major general in the army.

The few photographs we have of Mao with his children seem to reflect a relaxed relationship. But according to his daughter Li Na he was a strict father who 'didn't wish for us to become famous. He only wanted us to work with our own hands. He said he would be satisfied if we could become common labourers.' Mao's family life was perhaps not very warm. Like most elite offspring the Mao daughters became weekly boarders at school. Jiang Qing brought her half-sister to live in Zhongnanhai to care for them. Jiang herself was away in Moscow for medical treatment briefly in 1949, and for prolonged periods in 1952–3, 1955, and 1957. When she was in Beijing she was often bedridden in a separate apartment adjoining that of Mao. The couple's relationship is thought to have been poor. He did not encourage her return from Moscow and he had affairs with young women from his staff and from the military.

Economic policies

Of course Mao's main preoccupations were with national affairs, especially economic policy. The period 1949–53 laid the basis for recovery and development through the establishment of peace, civil order, and regular communications, all lacking in China throughout the first half of the century. The hyperinflation that had contributed significantly to the fall of the Guomindang was brought under control. During the civil war, the CCP had gained peasant support by redistributing land from landlords and sometimes rich peasant families to the poorer peasants in the areas it controlled. Land reform continued after the Party came to national power. Mao was at first associated with a comparatively moderate system under which the rich peasant economy would be preserved and production levels protected. In the end, a much tougher policy prevailed under which almost half China's cultivated acreage was redistributed. Class struggle was emphasized in land reform, old scores were settled, and there was considerable violence. It has been estimated that between one and two million landlords were killed.

The Soviet-style First Five Year Plan, which ran from 1953 to 1957, brought some real successes. There was enormous investment in infrastructure, especially in railways, bridges, and some key heavy industrial plants. Soviet technical aid played an important role. By 1956 both industry and trade had been brought under state control but former capitalists were compensated and the change was achieved with comparatively little disruption. The industrial growth rate was impressive though it started from a very small base. Economic progress was enough to raise public morale, and to create some improvement in the standard of living. There were remarkable advances in education and health in the urban areas but progress in the villages was more modest.

The pattern of initial moderation followed by radicalism seen in land reform also characterized the collectivization of agriculture. In the 1940s, Mao had implied that the socialization of industry and agriculture would not be carried out for some time. Agricultural collectivization was supposed to start slowly relying on voluntarism. Peasants were to be encouraged to pool their efforts and resources through mutual aid teams which would then be a foundation for small-scale cooperatives. However, in 1955, difficulties in procuring enough grain to feed the rapidly growing urban population led the communist leadership to put heavy pressure on the peasants to enter cooperatives. It was assumed that cooperatives would be more efficient producers than individual peasants and would be more easily persuaded to give up much-needed grain to the state. When the disruption and demoralization of over-rapid cooperativization brought about falls in production, the policy was briefly reversed and some cooperatives were even disbanded.

The reversal infuriated Mao, who saw it as a rejection of revolutionary policies. He convened a great conference of peasant activists and edited their favourable reports on the cooperatives into a volume entitled *Socialist Upsurge in the Chinese Countryside*. Bypassing the formal decision-making process, he called for the pace of cooperativization to be speeded up. By 1957, almost every peasant household had been pressed into higher-level co-ops in which land, livestock, and equipment were all collectively owned and remuneration depended on labour alone. Despite the speed of the process, production was not disrupted and this allowed Mao to claim a triumph. However, the basic problems in Chinese agriculture remained intractable. The amount of cultivated land per head of the population was one of the lowest in the world. Although the yield per hectare was high, labour productivity was low and it was hard for the peasants to produce much surplus on so little land whether collectivized or not. The state paid low prices for grain, there was too little investment in agriculture, and mechanization was difficult in such an intensive system. Basically, agriculture was squeezed to pay for the industrialization programme. Grain output did grow, but not as fast as envisaged in the plan.

During the period of the First Five Year Plan, every effort was made to preserve the appearance of a unified leadership under Mao's direction. It is now known that there were serious disagreements over various issues including the pace of the cooperativization of agriculture and the socialization of industry, but all this was successfully concealed at the time. The one major leadership purge that took place perhaps foreshadowed future events, although the details remain obscure. It involved Gao Gang, a Politburo member who had been leader of the Shaanxi Soviet before the arrival of the Long Marchers, and his associate Rao Shushi. Gao was the top official in the North-East China Region while Rao occupied an equivalent position in the East China Region. In 1953 both were transferred to senior posts in Beijing. Gao Gang had already incurred Mao's ire by conducting independent dealings with Stalin from his north-eastern stronghold. He had even concluded a trade treaty with the Soviet Union for his region before Mao agreed one for China as a whole. Nonetheless, it seems that Mao liked Gao and confided to him that he thought Liu Shaoqi and Zhou Enlai were over-cautious about the economy and collectivization. Mao also spoke about dropping some of his own frontline leadership tasks. Possibly encouraged by such talk, Gao and Rao are said to have plotted to take the places of Liu Shaoqi and Zhou Enlai. When this was reported back to Mao, they were challenged. Gao committed suicide and Rao was imprisoned.

The new society: assent and dissent

In the early 1950s, the new regime was rather successful at building popular support. Life in the first half of the twentieth century in a country almost continuously racked by war had been very difficult for the majority. The promise of strong and purposeful government and a better life to come was beguiling. Many people, especially the industrial workers who were enjoying considerable benefits in the new society, were convinced by the CCP's revolutionary message. Great effort was expended to make people feel part of 'New China'. Most of the population received some sort of 'political education' to explain and win support for the new government and its policies. This took place in the workplace, and in all sorts of organizations such as Peasant Associations, the Youth League, the Women's Federation, and even in the Young Pioneers, the communist children's organization.

On the other hand life was becoming very difficult for certain groups. Campaigns were launched successively against counter-revolutionaries, corrupt cadres, and businessmen accused of defrauding the state. Intellectuals underwent 'thought reform', designed to break their intellectual independence and to discredit all ideologies other than Marxism. They were made to feel guilty for their privileged past. At regular meetings, usually held at their place of work, they were required to consider their past actions and ideas and to make self-criticisms as well as criticisms of others. From the time of the Korean War life was particularly difficult for those who had connections with the United States, had been educated in mission schools, or had relatives in Taiwan. Individuals under attack were isolated, a painful state that imposed great psychological pressure in a society that seemed overwhelmingly united in the pursuit of economic progress, national self-determination, and socialism. Dissent resulted in tragic consequences for the dissidents and their families.

Mao followed campaigns that affected intellectuals with particular interest and sometimes intervened in them personally. In his 1940 essay 'On New Democracy' he had condemned Guomindang censorship, its suppression of intellectuals, and its oppressiveness towards all opponents. In Yan'an and in the first years in Beijing, his letters to established non-communist figures in the world of scholarship or the arts had often showed great respect. By contrast, in 1954 he made a vicious attack on Liang Shuming, a well-known liberal philosopher and writer and a friend of his former teacher, Yang Changji. Born in the same year as Mao, before 1949 Liang had advocated the blending of western-style democracy with eastern values. His crime on this occasion was to observe in a meeting that the life of a Chinese peasant was very hard and that workers had a better deal. Mao snatched up the microphone and shouted crude abuse at Liang calling him a heap of stinking bones. Although Liang was subsequently disgraced, he outlived Mao, dying in 1988. Perhaps, although Mao had lost his temper, he did not see him as a real threat. Later he was to say that even men like Liang should be allowed to spread their ideas. 'If they have something to fart about let them fart! If it's out, people can decide whether it is bad or good.'

Far more serious was the 1955 campaign personally orchestrated by Mao against Hu Feng, a leading CCP writer and Communist Party member. Hu had been bold enough to complain that Mao's 'Yan'an Talks' had been used to stifle all creativity in the arts. He was accused of leading a counter-revolutionary clique, arrested, and imprisoned. In the witch-hunt that followed, intellectuals labelled as his followers were persecuted and punished. Their families often shared their fates. Hu was not released until 1979, was rehabilitated in 1980, and lived until 1985.

Impact of Khrushchev's secret speech

Khrushchev's denunciation of Stalin at the Twentieth Congress of the Soviet Communist Party in February 1956 had enormous repercussions in China. Mao's attitudes to Stalin were complex. He can have had little love for the Soviet leader, despite the formal eulogy that he had written on the Soviet leader's death. As Mao himself commented, the Chinese Party had more than once experienced difficulties because of Stalin's interference, and the Chinese revolution won victory by acting contrary to Stalin's will. Stalin had many times backed Mao's rivals for the leadership of the CCP and had not seemed to want a communist victory in the Chinese civil war of 1946–9. Moreover, Mao harboured resentment about the terms of Soviet aid to China agreed in 1950 and Soviet behaviour during the Korean War. But in spite of all this, Mao had recognized Stalin as the leader of the socialist camp. He was dismayed that Khrushchev had failed to consult or even warn fraternal parties in advance about the disclosures he would make in his 'secret speech' and feared that the revelations would bring turmoil to the international communist movement.

The secret speech contained a strong attack on the cult of the individual. Khrushchev accused Stalin of demanding absolute submission to his opinions, ignoring the norms of Party life, and trampling on the Leninist principle of collective party leadership. There was already sensitivity about the cult of the individual in China. The Central Committee had clearly dissociated itself from some Soviet practices in 1949 by prohibiting the naming of towns, streets, or factories after living leaders. At Mao's suggestion, the Chinese leaders also made an anti-embalming pact, agreeing to be cremated after death to prevent their bodies becoming objects of veneration like Lenin's. Yet despite these precautions, Mao and his colleagues could hardly have failed to see that Mao, like Stalin, might be accused of putting himself above the Party.

The first public Chinese response to the secret speech came in a *People's Daily* editorial 'On the Historical Experience of the Dictatorship of the Proletariat', in April 1956, later to be regarded as an opening salvo in the Sino-Soviet split. The editorial reflects both Mao's ambivalence towards Stalin, and his critical attitude to the secret speech. It was not an out-and-out rejection of Khrushchev's denunciation. It even congratulated the Soviet people for launching a campaign against the cult of the individual and conceded that Stalin had made many mistakes. However, it insisted that his achievements were primary.

The autumn brought fresh drama in the Soviet bloc. The Polish United Workers Party tried to rid itself of leaders imposed on it by Stalin. Soviet military intervention in the Stalinist tradition seemed a real possibility. The CCP gave notice to Moscow that it strongly supported the Polish Party's right to determine its own affairs and opposed Soviet intervention. However, when the Hungarian Uprising took place in September, China supported Soviet intervention because the uprising was overtly anti-communist and the reformers wanted to leave the Warsaw pact.

The Hundred Flowers and the anti-rightist movement

Meanwhile, in China, possibly in response to questions under debate after Khrushchev's secret speech about how a socialist country should be run, Mao and some other Party leaders had begun to advocate greater intellectual freedom. In spring 1956, Mao raised the slogan 'Let a Hundred Flowers Bloom, Let a Hundred Schools of Thought Contend', urging that academic debate should take place without undue political restriction, and that the Party and officials should submit to public criticism. This seemed like an extraordinary reversal after the Hu Feng affair. It seems that Mao feared that economic development would be stalled if intellectuals, technical experts, and managers were held back by conformity or fear. The movement was intended to harness their energy and enthusiasm. When the intellectuals, mindful of the fate of Hu Feng and others, showed a very natural caution, Mao himself urged them to overcome their nervousness. He even attacked Party leaders who did not accept the Hundred Flowers. 'Shit or get off the pot' he shouted at the editor of the

People's Daily who had been slow to publish one of the key documents of the new policy.

Chinese leaders who had opposed the 'Hundred Flowers' initiative felt that the Hungarian Uprising of November 1956 confirmed their position on the dangers of allowing intellectual dissent but Mao at first stood firm. In February 1957, he delivered a key speech to a non-Party audience entitled 'On the Correct Handling of Contradictions', openly admitting that there was leadership opposition to the Hundred Flowers campaign and setting out a theory of contradictions to defend it. A distinction must be made, he argued, between 'contradictions among the people' and 'antagonistic contradictions'. If the former were ignored they could turn into the latter. Stalin had often confused these two types of contradiction and had thus failed to make the distinction between the enemy and the people. He had treated all those who made criticisms as enemies, even imprisoning or executing them. The CCP, said Mao, had recognized that this method was 'not suitable', yet it had sometimes made the same error. Mao admitted that 800,000 Chinese had been killed in drives against counter-revolutionaries but seemed to imply that the time for violent class struggle was now over. Most shockingly of all for the politically orthodox, Mao argued that there could be contradictions between the leaders and the led. It was quite possible for the Party and its leaders to commit errors and Party leaders however senior could not be immune from criticism. Party members and non-Party members had an equal right to criticize. Only through open debate could correct and incorrect ideas be distinguished.

Encouraged by what appeared to be a sustained relaxation, intellectuals, academics, scientists, technical experts, and managers began to attack the Party and its authoritarian role. They complained of narrow repressiveness and of inappropriate political interference in many spheres of life including education, research, industrial management, and construction. They also protested against low standards of living, political repression, and the slavish imitation of the Soviet Union. Mao's colleagues became more alarmed than ever, and Mao himself seems to have been at first taken aback, and then angered by this crescendo of resentful voices. In the summer, despite all Mao's promises about accepting criticism, a campaign of repression was launched, overseen by Deng Xiaoping, then a newly powerful figure as Deputy Premier, General Secretary of the CCP Central Committee, Director of the Organization Department, and Vice Chairman of the Central Military Commission. Over half a million 'rightists' were identified in universities, enterprises, and government offices including leading writers and thinkers. They were punished with varying degrees of severity, many being sent into exile or imprisonment for years. Their family members were discriminated against in education, job selection, and promotion.

Mao's motives in the Hundred Flowers movement and the 'anti-rightist movement' that followed have been much disputed. He has been accused of deliberately leading intellectuals into a trap; indeed, he himself later implied that it was part of his plan to entrap the 'poisonous weeds'. The documentary evidence is against this. Mao had pushed for the Hundred Flowers thaw in a mood of utopian optimism against considerable opposition. He believed that it would enable the Party to cooperate more fruitfully with the educated people whose skills it needed in order to speed the industrialization programme. The anti-rightist crackdown represented a defeat for this optimism and struck a blow to his prestige both with his colleagues, to whom his behaviour seemed rash and ill judged, and with the intellectuals, who felt that it had been treacherous. Educated Chinese now knew that expressing independent opinions honestly was dangerous, whereas sycophancy and conformity brought rewards. Mao's attitude to the intellectuals, always ambivalent, also seems to have become more firmly negative. Henceforth he frequently invoked the Petofi Circle, the group of writers who had first demanded reform in Hungary, to express concern about unreliable intellectuals. In February 1957 he had assured his colleagues that there would be no Petofi Circle in China; in 1963 he would warn writers that they might become such a grouping.

Leadership questions

The Eighth Party Congress was held in September 1956 after the secret speech and when the Hundred Flowers movement was already under way. It was the first since 1945, despite the constitutional requirement for five yearly congresses. Its very staging has been seen as marking the ascendancy of those like Liu Shaoqi and Deng Xiaoping who emphasized organization and legitimacy. The Congress agreed a number of measures which appeared to reduce Mao's role and stature. Photographic line-ups placed Liu Shaoqi beside Mao, thus confirming him as the heir apparent. Deng Xiaoping took on the newly created post of General Secretary of the Party. The post of honorary Party Chairman was created, but left vacant, apparently in preparation for Mao's eventual retirement. The new Party constitution stated that all important decisions should be taken collectively. The 1945 constitution had defined the Party's ideology as Marxism-Leninism Mao Zedong Thought. This reference to Mao Zedong Thought was dropped from the 1956 text. The Congress Documents are striking for the absence of the phrase 'under the correct leadership of the Communist Party led by Chairman Mao Zedong'. Such formulaic references had been the norm in all Party documents and would become so again from 1960, so that their omission in 1956 must have been deliberate.

In his report on the new constitution Deng Xiaoping rejected the concept of the infallible leader:

> One important contribution made by the 20th Congress of the Soviet Party was to alert us to the fact that the personality cult can lead to all sorts of disastrous consequences. Our party has always reckoned that any party or individual can have deficiencies or make mistakes; this point is now explicitly noted in the new draft of the

Party constitution. In this way our Party also repudiates the personality cult.

It is often assumed that the Eighth Congress represented an attempt by other CCP leaders, including Liu Shaoqi, Deng Xiaoping, and Peng Dehuai, to curb Mao's increasingly autocratic behaviour. The Red Guards who included this extract from Deng's report in a collection of his 'most criminal ideas' clearly saw it that way. Yet there are problems with such an interpretation. The Chinese Communist Youth League had dropped a similar reference to Mao Zedong Thought as early as 1953, presumably with Mao's agreement. The official CCP line supported by Mao was against the cult of the individual. Deng's comments merely echoed this position.

The Congress took place only months after the secret speech. It is possible that the language of its documents reflected a heightened sensitivity among all the leaders, including at the time Mao, to the fact that the CCP might be accused of practising the cult of the individual.

The preparations for Mao's retirement are compatible with his often expressed dislike of the day-to-day routines of government and his wish to retire to 'the second line', a term he used for the backstage position he thought would give him the time to think about long-term strategy. Other personnel decisions made at the Congress, in particular the appointment of the competent Deng Xiaoping as General Secretary, may have been designed to make this possible. The implication that Mao was too weak to fight back against Congress decisions with which he disagreed is at variance with the fact that, as events were to show, he still had formidable control over the Party. Whatever the real meaning of the Eighth Congress, any tensions that existed in this period were to be dwarfed by what happened in 1958 when Mao led China into the disastrous Great Leap Forward.

Chapter 5
The Great Leap Forward and its aftershocks

Mao's impatience with the pace of economic growth in China was increased by his second and final visit to the Soviet Union in November 1957. He obtained a promise of help with defence, and in particular nuclear technology, but it was made clear that other aid would be limited. Profound ideological differences began to emerge. Khrushchev stuck to the belief that he had expressed at the Soviet Party's Twentieth Congress that there should be peaceful coexistence with capitalist countries, arguing that in a nuclear age even local wars were too dangerous as they might escalate into nuclear conflict. Mao insisted that liberation wars were still necessary and could be limited.

The Chinese position reflected an ongoing feeling of vulnerability. Much of the new industrial development in China had been sited at great expense far in the interior to put it beyond the reach, it was hoped, of US bombs. China faced unyielding hostility from the United States, the Americans had given Taiwan the latest military equipment, and the American trade embargo had excluded China from world markets. Reliant on the Soviet nuclear deterrent, China was alarmed by any indication that Moscow might be 'going soft' rather than standing up to Washington. The

Russians were horrified by Mao's bravado when he insisted that a nuclear war would not be a total disaster. Khrushchev's return visit to Beijing in 1958 did nothing to heal the widening breach. Three weeks later, in brinkmanship which was perhaps intended as a lesson in anti-imperialist resolve for Moscow, the Chinese began shelling Guomindang-held islands in the Taiwan Straits. When a direct confrontation with the USA appeared to threaten, China backed down. After the conclusion of the crisis, belatedly in Chinese eyes, Khrushchev informed the USA that any attack on China would be regarded as an attack on the Soviet Union. Then in June 1959, the Soviets told the Chinese that they would not honour their promise to assist China with the development of a nuclear bomb because it would be contrary to their efforts to obtain a test ban treaty and bring about the relaxation of international tension. In 1959 and 1960 Mao was further infuriated by Moscow's failure to support either Chinese action in Tibet or China's stance in the Sino-Indian border dispute. The developing differences with the Soviet Union convinced Mao that China would have to depend more on its own efforts to industrialize and also inclined him to the belief that China should not slavishly follow the Soviet model. Mao revived the idea of an economic leap that he had first suggested in 1956. The Great Leap Forward was launched in the winter of 1957–8 with the aim of speeding up economic growth. Agricultural collectives were merged to make enormous new units called 'People's Communes'. Their size allowed them to mobilize tens of thousands of peasants in the winter months to work on construction projects. A huge expansion of irrigation was planned to protect against both flood and drought thus making farmland more productive. Local collectively owned small-scale industry, often using indigenous technology, would be encouraged. Modern industry was to be developed at the provincial level, making even the largely agricultural inland provinces self-sufficient in consumer goods. The intention was to eliminate transport bottle-necks and, through a dribble-down effect, to promote industrialization even in the most backward areas.

Social revolution was another objective of the Great Leap. The remuneration system in the People's Communes was at first extremely egalitarian. The patriarchal family came under new attack. Drives to get women involved in work outside the home were underpinned by the opening of communal kitchens and nurseries. The Great Leap involved a visionary attempt to use human labour power, of which China had so much, to replace the capital and the equipment that it lacked.

These were not necessarily irrational strategies; the problem lay in their hasty and inexpert implementation. Early in the campaign Mao warned against trying to go too fast, saying that economic laws exist objectively and cannot be diverted by man's will; however, he and the country at large soon abandoned this sort of caution. Aspirational but unrealistic economic targets such as catching up Britain within fifteen years were adopted.

Mao bears responsibility for the rhetoric of the Great Leap which invoked the importance of human will, enthusiasm, and dedication, and tended to condemn expert opinion as dogmatism. His desire to win over planners and managers manifested in the Hundred Flowers movement disappeared; now he urged that people should not 'fear professors'. He likened the problem of achieving development to that of fighting a war, he spoke of the necessity of permanent revolution, and his speeches reflected a growing impatience with the sober advice of technical experts. The Great Leap was characterized by an extreme anti-expert bias. It was better to be 'red' than 'expert', and engineers who protested that production targets were impractical or mentioned the technical limitations of machinery could find themselves accused of counter-revolutionary behaviour.

The coming of disaster

Great Leap policies affected everyone's lives. The extreme egalitarianism of the remuneration system in the People's

Communes gave peasants too little economic incentive. The massive water control projects and the rural industries that the communes were supposed to facilitate were often ill advised, and sometimes diverted too much peasant labour away from grain production. The naive notion that steel was the basis of all industrialization and the determination to increase China's output led to the massively wasteful 'backyard furnace movement'. People were called on to give up 'scrap iron'—in fact usually their precious pots, pans, and tools—which enthusiastic activists with no experience of metallurgy all too often reduced to low-grade scrap when they attempted to produce steel.

Reliable statistics were among the first casualties of the Great Leap. Cadres feared to admit that they had not reached their targets, and as one unit reported record outputs, another would feel challenged to claim even more exaggerated achievements. Despite the assignment of so many male peasants to make steel or to work in industry, it was claimed that grain outputs had doubled in 1958. Similarly impressive figures were put forward for industry.

Analysis of revised figures for industry shows initial growth that was not maintained. Indeed growth fell sharply away and production did not recover its 1960 level until 1965. Losses in agriculture were far more serious. Revised figures show that what had been hailed as a bumper harvest in 1958 was in fact only 2.6 per cent greater than that of 1957. Grain output then suffered catastrophic declines for two consecutive years. In 1960 output was 29 per cent lower than in 1958. Only in 1965 did grain output come near to recovering the 1957 level. Meanwhile the state failed to make an appropriate response until 1961. Determined to continue to feed the urban areas and to supply industrial needs, it took over 17.4 per cent of the crop from the peasants in 1957, 20.9 per cent in 1958, 28 per cent in the terrible year of 1959, and 21 per cent in 1960. China even remained a net exporter of grain up to and including 1960, the worst harvest year, and began substantial imports of food grain only in 1961. Predictably the result of this ruthless grain procurement by the state in what was still a largely self-sufficient agricultural economy was an appalling famine. Death rates shot up while birth rates plummeted. Between 20 and 30 million deaths—some estimates go much higher—resulted from the direct and indirect effects of the famine.

Famine theorists have shown that large-scale famines are not brought about merely by a dearth of food; poor governance and access and entitlement to food are also important factors. Prompt reactions to the first signs of famine are vital if the effects of shortage are to be mitigated. In its early years Mao's regime had almost banished starvation by giving the poorest peasants access to land, increasing production, and distributing relief grain. In the Great Leap period, euphoria, ignorance, and fear inhibited ameliorative action when famine first began to strike.

Mao, as the chief architect of the policies that produced the famine and of a political culture in which even his oldest comrades increasingly feared to bring up unpalatable truths, bears responsibility for one of the greatest disasters in human history. Zhou Enlai, who had expressed reservations about the Great Leap Forward at the beginning of 1958, had been forced to make an abject self-criticism for his economic conservatism, even offering his resignation. The veteran Party economist Chen Yun, a believer in the orthodox planned economy, was another doubter. The anti-expert ethos that had prevailed since the anti-rightist movement weakened his position. In early 1959, he made a brave speech asserting that economic growth required attention to safe working conditions and quality engineering, and depended not just on political awareness, but also on technical skill. Interestingly, although he would be criticized for the speech years later in the Cultural Revolution, it did not result in immediate trouble. Other leaders such as Liu Shaoqi and Deng Xiaoping seem initially to have offered Mao their support for the Great

Leap. However, the heady optimism that prevailed in 1958 rapidly dissipated in 1959 as knowledge of the real situation reached the leaders.

In June 1959, in the midst of the disaster, Mao left Beijing to inspect conditions in the provinces. He had handed over the chairmanship of the People's Republic to Liu Shaoqi in April, although he remained the Party chairman. His trip was perhaps understood by some to mark his long-promised retreat to the second line. In Hubei province conditions were so bad that even the state guesthouse at which he stayed with his entourage could serve no meat. In Hunan he went to his home village after an absence of thirty-two years. He visited his parents' graves and then chatted to relatives, villagers, and local officials. Reports of these talks show that he must have had some insight into what was going on. He chided officials who gave him favourable reports of agricultural production, telling them not to exaggerate. In the evening the villagers complained to him that production was down and that they had had to give up their pots and pans to the backyard furnaces.

The purge of Peng Dehuai

The following month, Mao moved on to Jiangxi province, where a Central Committee plenum had been arranged for July in the mountain resort of Lushan. Some of the other leaders had also been travelling in various parts of the countryside. What they had seen had made them question the Great Leap but they were afraid to say anything that might get back to Mao. However, the minister of defence, Marshal Peng Dehuai, had decided to speak out. Like Mao, Peng was from a peasant background in Hunan province. Their association went back to their guerrilla days in Jinggangshan. Peng had served with distinction in both the war of resistance and the civil war, and had commanded the Chinese forces in Korea. He was a blunt-speaking soldier whose knowledge of military technology had made him acutely aware of China's backwardness. He had complained about Mao's personality cult and disapproved of Mao's affairs with young women from the military. He himself was popular in the army for his simple lifestyle.

Peng had visited his own and Mao's home districts early in 1959. Horrified to see untilled fields and starving peasants, he sent cables to Beijing about conditions. Just before the Lushan plenum he had spent six weeks in Eastern Europe and had met Khrushchev. In small group discussions at the start of the plenum, Peng criticized Great Leap policies. He also pointed out that production in Mao's home village had increased with the help of large loans from the state. When Mao professed ignorance of this, Peng said he did not believe him, thus implying that the Chairman had lied. Peng also wrote a personal letter to Mao observing that there had been more losses than gains in the Great Leap and that steel production had been exaggerated. He condemned the 'leftist' mistakes of the campaign, saying they could also be described as 'petty bourgeois'. He averred that the collective leadership, including Mao, should take responsibility.

Mao was outraged. He felt that Peng's attack was directed at him personally and prepared an immediate counter-attack. First he had the letter copied and distributed to all the delegates. The fact that Mao himself had ordered the distribution of the letter and that the criticisms of the Great Leap it contained were no stronger than what Mao had already said led some to suppose the Chairman would allow an open discussion. They were soon disabused. In a furious speech Mao defended the communes. He warned that although he never attacked first, when he came under fire, he would always counter-attack. Then he issued an ultimatum; he would go up into the mountains and start a new guerrilla war if the army followed Peng. The marshal exploded with anger and accused Mao of being a despot, like Stalin in his later years, ready to sacrifice human life in pursuit of impossible targets.

At the Politburo meeting which followed, Mao took advantage of the fact that Khrushchev had just launched a public attack on the Chinese communes to accuse Peng of having plotted with the Soviet leader. Mao and Peng swore furiously at each other. Peng protested that his letter had been intended only for Mao and that he had carried out no factional activities. Mao of course prevailed. Zhou Enlai and others joined the attack. Peng was soon isolated. Only his fellow marshal, Zhu De, tried to defend him.

Peng was subsequently replaced as minister of defence by another marshal, Lin Biao. Both Mao and Liu Shaoqi frequently asserted that Peng had acted as a Soviet agent at Lushan. Later in 1959, on what was to be his final visit to Beijing, Khrushchev urged Mao to restore Peng to his positions. The intervention was hardly likely to have helped Peng. Yet for some years Peng's treatment was relatively mild. He retained his Party membership but lived under house arrest on the outskirts of Beijing. He cultivated his garden and was sometimes visited by other leaders. In 1965, Mao sent for him again. Having grudgingly admitted to Peng that at Lushan, 'from the perspective of today, the truth may have been on your side', Mao asked him to take charge of a new programme of economic development in inland China. This partial rehabilitation did not last long. Peng was arrested by Red Guards in 1966, tortured and interrogated, and subsequently held in prison until his death from cancer in 1974. His posthumous rehabilitation was announced by Deng Xiaoping in 1978. Deng stated that Mao's vilification of Peng in 1959 as the leader of an 'anti-Party clique' had been 'entirely wrong', and that it had 'undermined intra-Party democracy'. Paying tribute to Peng, Deng said, 'He cared about the masses, and was never concerned about his own advantage. He was never afraid of difficulties, neither of carrying heavy loads.'

Retreat from the Great Leap

Ironically, Peng's stand against Mao made retreat from the Great Leap all the more difficult because Mao's pride was at stake.

Moves to modify and stabilize communes in spring 1959 were replaced by an attempt to revive Great Leap policies in 1960. A real retreat finally began in 1961, despite a continuing rhetoric glorifying the Great Leap. By this time the true magnitude of the famine was apparent to the leadership. Liu Shaoqi, Zhou Enlai, and Deng Xiaoping directed the adjustments, which involved a reduction in the size of communes and considerable modification of their early egalitarian policies. In some cases, peasant households even regained control over the land from the collective. In 1962, Mao called an expanded Central Committee work conference in Beijing attended by 7,000 cadres. He hoped the meeting would stop the retrenchment which he perceived as a retreat from socialism. In the event, grass-roots cadres were so eloquent in their condemnation of Great Leap policies that Mao was forced to make a rather perfunctory self-criticism. After the meeting Mao withdrew to south China for several months leaving Liu, Zhou, and Deng in charge of affairs in Beijing. The economy gradually recovered and, although rationing remained, by 1963 food was becoming more plentiful. Even policies towards literature, the arts, and education were somewhat relaxed.

Meanwhile the Sino-Soviet dispute, which had been festering since Khrushchev's secret speech in 1956, finally became an open split in 1960. The Russians cancelled their aid to China and withdrew their experts and advisers. Many were glad to go because their restraining advice had been rejected since the beginning of the Great Leap Forward. Their withdrawal was a new blow to the Chinese economy; some construction sites where Soviet expertise had been indispensable now lay idle. However, the Russian withdrawal, together with some serious natural disasters in 1960 and 1961, gave Mao a useful scapegoat for the trouble the economy was in.

From 1962 to 1965, China enjoyed comparative political calm. Yet there were rumbles of dissension. At first, Mao accepted the retrenchment measures, but in a speech at Beidaihe in the summer of 1962, he insisted that the collectives must be preserved and that class struggle must not be forgotten. Contending explanations of the disaster years were an indication of tension. Liu Shaoqi said that 70 per cent of the Great Leap Forward problems were due to human error and 30 per cent to the weather. Mao insisted that it was the other way round. A Socialist Education Campaign that began under Liu Shaoqi's direction in 1963 was designed to strengthen collectivization by cleaning up corruption in the administration of collective accounts, communal granaries, public property, and work points. Work teams of cadres and students from the cities went to the countryside to carry out the work; it was felt that such outsiders would not be 'contaminated' by local interests and that the experience would be good for their own socialist education. By 1964 Mao was unhappy with the direction taken by the campaign. He thought too much effort was being put into unearthing the insignificant misdemeanours of rural cadres and too little into seeking out the 'capitalistic' elements among the peasants. He claimed that his injunction 'Never forget class struggle' had been forgotten.

The Sino-Soviet split

The Sino-Soviet split is an essential background to understanding Mao's evolving ideas in this period. Relations between the two parties worsened after the withdrawal of Soviet aid in 1960. Until 1963, however, they used surrogates in launching attacks on each other. Beijing blasted Yugoslav revisionism rather than the Soviet Union while Moscow abused Albania rather than China. All this came to an end when the Soviet Union signed the nuclear test ban treaty in summer 1963. Mao had once proclaimed that the atom bomb was a paper tiger, but this was clearly bravado. He wanted nuclear weapons and was infuriated by what he saw as an attempt to block China developing them. From September 1963 to July 1964, the CCP issued a series of nine bitter letters directly attacking the Soviet Party ideologically and politically. Written in the name of the Chinese Central Committee, these may be taken as expressing

Mao's increasingly negative views of political and economic developments in the USSR. In 1964 China tested its first atom bomb, a feat applauded as a great triumph all over the country.

Mao no longer believed that a socialist revolution guaranteed a continuous advance towards communism. Rather he argued that class struggle must continue under socialism as the only protection against the restoration of capitalism. He came to regard the Soviet Party as a revisionist force engaged in just such a restoration and he increasingly feared that the same fate could befall the Chinese Party if steps were not taken to avoid it. The fall of Khrushchev in 1964 created considerable excitement in China, but in the end did nothing to reassure Mao, who condemned the new Soviet leadership as offering 'Khrushchevism without Khrushchev'. The spectacle of the Kremlin coup may also have increased Mao's paranoia about his own position and his relationships with senior colleagues.

The Sino-Soviet split left China isolated internationally, as all the communist countries of Eastern Europe, except tiny Albania, sided with Moscow. The Vietnam War again brought a conflict involving the USA close to China's borders. Chinese propaganda claimed, 'We have friends all over the world', and China began a friendship offensive with various countries in the Third World especially in the newly independent countries of Africa. But Mao clearly felt exposed. He viewed the international situation as unstable enough to justify massive expenditure invested in the 'third front', a policy under which much strategic industry was transferred to the south-western provinces such as Sichuan where it would be less vulnerable to foreign attack and where supplies for the Vietnamese war effort could conveniently be produced.

Mao's increasing isolation

Socially, Mao was now more than ever dependent for company on his bodyguards and on those who attended to his needs and pleasures. His old comrades were nervous of him, his children had grown up, and his relationship with Jiang Qing was volatile. She was exacting and neurotic. Her health and his infidelities had led to an estrangement in the 1950s, yet she had flown to be at Mao's side when the row with Peng Dehuai broke out at Lushan. This did not produce a permanent marital reconciliation, but their political relationship strengthened as their personal one waned. In 1966, she would move out of his household, yet he had already by then begun to allow her some political oversight of cultural affairs and during the Cultural Revolution he used her in many ways and permitted her to play a major political role. In 1961, Mao made the strangely quixotic gesture of arranging for his former wife, He Zizhen, to visit him when he was holidaying in Lushan. He chatted to her for a while, and after she had left, he chain-smoked for a long time. He had been distressed to see how old she looked and asked his doctor about her condition and its treatment. His reaction was perhaps connected to intimations of his own mortality as he struggled with minor ailments and his usual insomnia. He was more than ever addicted to sleeping pills.

Although propaganda emphasized Mao's frugality, his life in Zhongnanhai was comfortable enough. His bedroom was dominated by an enormous bed covered in heaps of books and papers and surrounded by bookshelves which were also piled high with books. He received guests in a room similarly full of books that resembled a study. He scrutinized a huge number of reports and other documents, but also remained a devoted reader of the Chinese classics, of which he collected beautiful editions. In the provinces he stayed in well-appointed guesthouses. Like Zhongnanhai, each of these had a heated pool. Swimming was his relaxation. He liked to spend long periods in south China where the climate suited him. His remoteness from the details of policy implementation now meant that he could put forward new ideas and policies without having to grapple with the practical problems of making them work. Moreover, having withdrawn to the 'second line', deliberately distancing himself from day-to-day affairs in

Beijing, he could accuse his colleagues of ignoring him when he disapproved of what they were doing.

The cult of Mao and its uses

In 1964 the cult of Mao was intensified. His name was mentioned with ever greater frequency in broadcasts. Chinese radio increased its output of revolutionary songs vaunting Mao's leadership while western classical music went off the air. His *Selected Works* was reissued, and a collection of extracts from his writings edited for the use of the army by Lin Biao appeared. Later editions were bound in a red vinyl cover and within two years a copy of *Quotations from Chairman Mao*, better known in English as *The Little Red Book*, would be owned and carried by everyone in China as the study of Mao's thought became obligatory.

In retrospect, this new elevation of Mao may be seen as a response to Khrushchev's fall and to Mao's concern about opposition to his ideas among his colleagues. In January 1965, Edgar Snow asked Mao if a cult of personality was being fostered in China. Having admitted that there was some basis for saying so, Mao suggested that Khrushchev had fallen because he had no cult of personality at all. The implication was that Mao regarded his cult as a protection.

At this point, ordinary Chinese were not aware of differences among the leadership of the CCP; nor, probably, did his colleagues realize how fundamentally Mao felt alienated from them. His anger and his conviction that China was being led into revisionism would soon lead him to launch a new campaign. For the first time, instead of trying to unite a majority of the Party leadership around his ideas, he would strike at the Party itself. To do this he would rely mainly on the support of young people brought up to consider him infallible. The new campaign would claim as its victims almost all Mao's old comrades and would thus leave him ever more heavily dependent on sycophants who drew their authority from their relationship with him.

Chapter 6
The Cultural Revolution: it's right to rebel

In its first fifteen years the Chinese communist government under Mao's leadership had brought the whole of mainland China under one effective government for the first time since 1911, established an administration whose writ ran even into remote villages, achieved economic and infrastructural growth, and brought about improvements in living standards and life expectancy. Literacy, education, and health standards had all seen remarkable rises, especially in the urban areas. The regime had survived both a direct clash with American military power in Korea, and the loss of Soviet aid after 1960. It had won considerable popular support on the basis of this record and through the patriotic nationalism that the Party fostered in all its educational and political work. The terrible post-Great Leap famine had been a severe setback but knowledge of its appalling scale had been successfully restricted to the top leadership. By the mid-1960s food supplies were again adequate, economic growth had been resumed, and confidence was returning.

However, by 1965, Mao was becoming increasingly disillusioned with the way Chinese society was developing. He believed that socialism was endangered by the measures introduced to restore the economy after the Great Leap disasters, in particular the introduction of material incentives in industry and the modifications to the collective system in agriculture. In retrospect, he had become critical even of development prior to the Great Leap Forward, viewing it as urban biased and inclined to promote the formation of a new communist elite. His criticism found voice in his 1965 Directive on Health. He accused the Ministry of Public Health of working only for 15 per cent of the population while the broad masses of the peasants got no medical treatment. 'First they don't have any doctors; second they don't have any medicine.' Sarcastically he asked, 'why not change its name to the Ministry of Urban Health . . . or even to Ministry of Urban Gentlemen's Health?' In education he urged that the curriculum should be simplified and more emphasis should be placed on practical work. Mao's analysis that the Soviet Party's ideology and policy were no longer revolutionary, that they had become revisionist, and his growing anger at the Soviet treatment of China also fed his concern that China itself might turn away from revolutionary politics and become revisionist.

Most of all Mao resented what he saw as his colleagues' reluctance to take his opinions seriously. Perhaps he even worried that his leadership faced a real challenge. Stalin's fate made clear that a leader's legacy could be rejected once he was dead, but Khrushchev's overthrow in 1964 showed that this could happen to a living leader. As the different strands of his unease came together, Mao seems to have concluded that the idea of his withdrawal to the second line had been a mistake. He decided to initiate one last campaign to safeguard his revolutionary legacy. This was the titanic struggle which became known as the Cultural Revolution. Its violent and chaotic phase lasted until from 1966 to 1969 when Mao pronounced it complete, although, to the horror of many, he sometimes said that there would be a need for further cultural revolutions in future. The post-Mao leadership redefined the Cultural Revolution as the 'ten years of catastrophe', the period from 1966 to 1976, in order to discredit the leftist policies of the 1970s, and this periodization is now quite generally adopted.

Although in retrospect the Cultural Revolution was clearly in part a leadership power struggle, it was not an orthodox purge. Mao did not simply use the Party or state apparatus to get rid of those he saw as his opponents, instead he mobilized the young people of China as 'Red Guards' and, astonishingly, allowed them to attack the Party apparatus. Different factions in the leadership manipulated these 'mass organizations', but often lost control of them. The movement was at first characterized by substantial spontaneity. Because Mao said that members of mass organizations should be able to write and produce newspapers, hundreds of unofficial newssheets were produced in this period. Many of the young activists who threw themselves into this new revolution were attracted by what they saw as a grass-roots movement which would at last lift the heavy hand of bureaucratic Party control.

Hai Rui, an allegory?

The first salvo of the Cultural Revolution was an attack on the play *Hai Rui Dismissed from Office*. This story of an upright Ming dynasty official who was sacked when he remonstrated with the emperor had been dramatized by Wu Han, a deputy mayor of Beijing and a leading historian. Ironically, Mao himself had inspired interest in Hai Rui several years earlier by urging that more should be written about him. When the play was first staged in early 1961, Mao expressed approval and dismissed Jiang Qing's charge that it was a thinly veiled defence of Peng Dehuai.

By 1965, however, Mao realized he could use the allegation. An attack on Wu Han would be an indirect attack on the mayor of Beijing, Peng Zhen, who was also deputy head of the Secretariat of the Chinese Communist Party, and in Mao's eyes associated with attempts to sideline him. Mao sent Jiang Qing to Shanghai where she commissioned a young polemicist, Yao Wenyuan, to write an attack on the play. Mao himself revised the draft and it appeared in the Shanghai press at the beginning of November. Ignorant of the link with Mao, Peng Zhen blocked its publication in Beijing until the end of the month. After an intervention by Zhou Enlai, presumably prompted by Mao, it was finally reprinted in the *People's Daily*. Peng was head of a small group that was supposed to oversee a revolution in culture. Unwisely, in February, he used this position to try to defend Wu Han. He admitted that Wu had made political mistakes but criticized Yao's article saying that such a political attack was inappropriate in an academic debate.

Mao had already told close followers that he now saw the play as an allegorical attack on his leadership, but he waited until late March, when Liu Shaoqi had left China for a month of state visits to other countries in Asia, to launch an open attack on Wu Han and his 'backer' Peng Zhen. At Mao's instigation, the Secretariat of the Central Committee (chaired by Deng Xiaoping) prepared the case against Peng. In April, Peng was denounced at a meeting of the Standing Committee of the Politburo in Hangzhou and in May he was indicted, along with three other high-ranking leaders who Mao had decided should go, at an enlarged meeting of the Politburo in Beijing stacked with Mao's supporters. The charge was that they had formed 'an anti-Party clique'. Although Mao did not attend this meeting, it was a key event. Ranking leaders, including Liu Shaoqi, Deng Xiaoping, and Zhou Enlai, did not attempt to stand up to Mao and allowed themselves to be manipulated into supporting charges against old comrades which they cannot sincerely have believed.

Mao's attack on senior colleagues broadens

The Standing Committee meeting announced the launch of a 'Great Proletarian Cultural Revolution' and referred to 'people in authority taking the capitalist road', the formulation that would later be used to describe Liu Shaoqi. The body that emerged from it, the new Cultural Revolution Group, in theory reported to the Standing Committee of the Politburo, but in fact was frequently to act as an alternative power source. Its members, although prominent, were not top-ranking leaders. All were radical Mao supporters. They included Chen Boda (a former secretary to Mao), Kang Sheng (the secret police chief who had supported Mao's marriage to Jiang Qing in Yan'an), Jiang Qing herself, her Shanghai protégé Yao Wenyuan, and another Shanghai leftist, Zhang Chunqiao.

Now distrustful of his Party colleagues whom he saw as part of a new elite, Mao turned to China's young people, and above all to students, to bring about the changes he wanted. In late May, Nie Yuanzi, a Beijing University teacher, put up a wall poster attacking the university president and urging students and staff to 'eliminate all demons and monsters and carry the socialist revolution through to the end'. It later emerged that Kang Sheng had sent his wife to offer Nie Yuanzi's protest high-level support. Knowing nothing of this, the university authorities instantly moved to condemn the poster, but on 1 June Mao endorsed it and it was broadcast by radio stations throughout the county. With this sort of encouragement, students and young people everywhere began to protest on the streets, to write wall posters, and to form Red Guard groups as their schools closed. All sorts of grievances emerged. Common themes were tyrannical Party leaders, nepotism, cronyism, and poor teaching, but local and individual issues also fuelled direct action.

Anxious that China was descending into chaos, Liu Shaoqi rang Mao in Hangzhou to ask him to come back to Beijing and take charge of the movement. When Mao demurred, Liu and Deng Xiaoping flew south to ask what action they should take. Mao repeated that they should do as they thought best, but he did not oppose their suggestion of sending teams of Party and Communist

Youth League members to the major campuses to restore order. Radical students were already organizing struggle meetings against their teachers, forcing them to kneel for long hours in dunce's caps in front of crowds of students and to make grovelling apologies for past 'reactionary' behaviour. The work teams that were sent in to impose order held their own struggle sessions and attempted to punish the radicals. Sharp conflicts broke out in most universities.

In July, newspapers all over China carried pictures of Mao's latest exploit. He had swum 9 miles across the Yangzi at Wuhan, a remarkable feat for a 72-year-old man even with the current in his favour. The clear message was that he was still vigorous and fully in charge. The publicity was timed to coincide with Mao's return to Beijing. Back in the capital he announced that 'to rebel is justified', a four-character phrase that the Red Guards would often use to legitimize their activities in the three following years. Mao also condemned the record of the work teams and these were withdrawn from all campuses.

At a plenum meeting of the Central Committee on 1 August, Mao interrupted Liu Shaoqi's opening speech with a public denunciation of the work teams which he accused of opposing proletarian revolution. Liu, who must by now have recognized that he had been set up, began to make muted self-criticisms. On 5 August, Mao put up his own wall poster outside the offices of the Central Committee. Under the dramatic heading 'Bombard the Headquarters', he alleged that certain leading comrades who had already acted against him in 1962 (over the modification of the communes) and in 1964 (over the Socialist Education Campaign) were now opposing the Cultural Revolution and trying to set up a bourgeois dictatorship. When the plenum elected the new Politburo, Liu Shaoqi had slipped from second to ninth in the new rank order. Lin Biao, the minister of defence who had replaced Peng Dehuai, was now in second place to Mao.

The plenum also approved the 'Sixteen Points', a new document that gave some idea of the course that the Cultural Revolution would take. It was to be a movement of the masses in which they would liberate themselves. The target of the movement should be those in authority who were taking the capitalist road. Old ideas, culture, customs, and habits were to be resisted and education, literature, and art transformed. Mao Zedong Thought should be taken as the guide to action. Some points, all too often ignored in the heat of the movement, counselled comparative moderation. Violence was not to be used in debate. The strictest care was to be taken to distinguish between 'the anti-Party, anti-socialist rightists and those who support the Party and socialism but have said or done something wrong or have written some bad articles...'. The great majority of cadres were 'good' or 'comparatively good'. Significantly, the Cultural Revolution in the armed forces was to be carried out under separate authority. In fact the military and nuclear weapons sites remained off limits to the 'revolutionary masses' throughout the Cultural Revolution.

The Red Guards

The Red Guard movement now took off. In their home towns Red Guards raided private houses and confiscated or destroyed property defined as representing old or bourgeois culture. Often they ransacked their own homes, burning books and photographs and smashing possessions. Having detained, interrogated, ill treated, and even beaten leaders supposed to represent bourgeois authority, they dragged them to struggle meetings where they were publicly humiliated. Some were beaten to death and others committed suicide.

Between mid-August and November Mao expressed his support and approval of the Red Guard movement by appearing at eight mass rallies in Beijing. Young people from all over China chanted slogans and wept hysterically on glimpsing their beloved Chairman. He waved in response. From the autumn, Red Guards were allowed free passage on the railways and many travelled from one end of China to the other 'exchanging revolutionary experience' and swapping Mao badges.

Red Guard organizations tended to divide into factions and fight amongst themselves. Those with 'good class backgrounds', the children of peasants, workers, and old revolutionaries whose families had benefited from the communist revolution, were usually less radical and tried to defend the status quo. Those with 'bad class backgrounds'—the children of the pre-revolutionary elite, landlord families, intellectuals, and those with connections in Taiwan or abroad—resented the discrimination to which they had been subject. They tended to be very radical. Yet they were subject to attack from other groups precisely because their background was questionable. All groups justified their policies and actions with reference to Mao's works. When Mao gave a clear order they tried to obey it. Much of the time, however, Mao was careful to hide his hand. His comments were Delphic in their ambiguity leaving Red Guard organizations considerable room to act on their own initiative. Communist leaders vying for power or survival whether at local or national level tried to manipulate Red Guard groups, sometimes through their own children. Like gang members anywhere, Red Guard organizations developed their own rivalries and antagonisms, albeit with ideological rationalizations. In some cases, they imprisoned, tortured, and even murdered each other with disturbing brutality.

The Mao cult became more intense than ever. Between 1966 and 1968, 150 million copies of Mao's *Selected Works* and 740 million copies of the *Little Red Book* were printed (see Figure 9). Every working day and every meeting included time spent reading from Mao's works. His picture hung in every room and every office. All newspapers and all books used Mao quotations as headers. His picture was so ubiquitous, it became dangerous to use old newspapers to light fires or wrap rubbish without checking for

9. Cultural Revolution poster—Chairman Mao is the Red Sun in our Hearts

them. Disrespect for Mao's image could be punished by imprisonment or worse. Ignorant of the details of China's revolutionary history, the young Red Guards idolized Mao as China's only saviour while they ill treated and interrogated others who also had dedicated their lives to the revolution. Intellectuals, teachers, and old revolutionaries alike were accused of being bourgeois and ill treated, imprisoned, beaten to death. The veteran author Lao She was one of many driven to suicide. Victims who survived joined in the adulation of Mao in often vain attempts to protect themselves.

Between 1966 and 1969, even the most senior of the old Party leaders were under pressure. The 80-year-old Marshal Zhu De was denounced in wall posters although Mao at least forbade physical violence against him. When other leaders such as Peng Dehuai, the veteran He Long, and the vice premiers Lo Ruiqing and Liu Dingyi were dragged before struggle meetings, Mao left the masses to do as they saw fit. He did not order their ill treatment but neither did he intervene to prevent it. At a lower level few leaders escaped terrible experiences whether in government offices, factories, or schools.

From late 1966 there were 'seizures of power' when Red Guard organizations took control at workplaces including even some central ministries in Beijing. In Shanghai, the Scarlet Guards, an alliance of industrial workers and students, organized strikes. Then their rivals, the more radical Red Rebels, seized control of the Shanghai municipal government in February 1967 and set up the 'Shanghai commune' as a new government. At this point, however, Mao drew back from the abyss, condemning the commune and the free elections it had announced. Instead, the approved model was the 'three in one committee', an alliance of revolutionary rebels and representatives of the army and veteran cadres. These were to replace old authorities such as city and provincial governments and enterprise managements. Such committees frequently came under violent attack from the radicals but they were gradually formed throughout the country.

Mao was not yet willing to abandon the radical Red Guard groups. When some old veterans in the Politburo, led by Marshal Ye Jianying, were emboldened enough by Mao's rejection of the Shanghai commune initiative to condemn the takeovers and the attacks on senior revolutionaries, Mao summoned them for a midnight telling off and once more threatened to start a new guerrilla war. The veterans' action was dubbed 'the February adverse current' and attacked in the media. However, only one of the participants was actually purged. He had insulted Jiang Qing by comparing her to the Empress Wu, a hate figure in Chinese history. This was still a step too far. With the other veterans, Mao attempted to build bridges.

Chaos continued throughout 1967. Some Red Guard groups seized arms from the military and the scale of violence increased. In July serious armed conflict broke out in Wuhan and there were thousands of deaths in vicious factional fighting in many other provinces. Guangxi and Guangdong were the scenes of terrible battles. Hundreds of bodies tossed into the river were eventually recovered in Hong Kong, bringing China bad publicity abroad. In August, attacks on foreign embassies and the sacking of the British mission in Beijing seriously compromised China's already difficult foreign relations.

A new campaign against Liu Shaoqi began in 1967. In April, Liu's wife Wang Guangmei was dragged from their house and taken to a struggle meeting in Qinghua University. She was forced to appear before thousands of Red Guards in a silk dress, high heels, and a necklace made of ping pong balls, a cruel mockery of the pearls that she had worn (against Jiang Qing's advice) on a state visit to Indonesia (see Figure 10). In July, Red Guards again

10. Wang Guangmei, wife of Liu Shaoqi, humiliated by Red Guards

raided the leadership compound and ill treated Liu and his wife over several hours. Liu sent his resignation as head of state to Mao. He and his wife were kept separately under house arrest while their children were sent to the countryside. According to evidence produced by the post-Mao leadership, a group set up to investigate him was headed by Jiang Qing. Liu was accused not only of having 'led an attack on the proletarian headquarters of Mao Zedong' after the Great Leap, but of having betrayed the revolution long before in the 1920s and 1930s. Deng Xiaoping was also put under house arrest. Red Guards assembled a collection of his 'criminal thoughts' which included his 1956 condemnation of the cult of the individual. With Mao's cult in full flow, this was now considered counter-revolutionary.

The rise of the radicals

The campaigns against Liu, Deng, and many other senior revolutionaries were largely masterminded by members of the Cultural Revolution Small Group, notably Jiang Qing, Kang Sheng, Chen Boda, and Zhang Chunqiao. They also instigated attacks on officials, intellectuals, and people from the world of the arts and of literature. Jiang Qing would later say in her own defence that she had been Chairman Mao's dog and that when he told her to bite someone, she bit. It is true that senior veterans could not have been attacked without Mao's acquiescence, but the radicals certainly took the chance to settle old scores. Jiang Qing was able to wreak revenge on those who had once denied her any public role. She was also anxious to silence her associates from 1930s Shanghai and arranged for their houses to be searched for old letters and photographs. One of them, a well-known film director, was arrested and later died in prison. If made public, details of Jiang Qing's life as a minor starlet in her youth would have upset her remake as a revolutionary leader with a special relationship to the Red Guards. After Mao's death, Jiang Qing was blamed for so many of the outrages of the Cultural Revolution that it is clear she was a scapegoat, yet most witnesses

向江青同志学习 向江青同志致敬

11. Jiang Qing Cultural Revolution poster with caption saying 'Learn from Jiang Qing, pay respects to Jiang Qing'

agree that she showed a particular malevolence towards her victims (see Figure 11).

In the summer of 1967, Mao made a lengthy tour of the provinces. Appalled by the turmoil and destruction everywhere, he ordered the army to restore order and called for the formation of the three in one revolutionary committees to be speeded up. Over the next year these 'grand alliances' were gradually set up to govern every province and manage every enterprise. However, clashes between different factions of Cultural Revolution activists continued and now that many of these were armed with weapons taken from military stores or even trains transporting arms to Vietnam, such incidents were often bloody, with high casualties. Despite attempting to curb the worst excesses of the radicals, Mao still vacillated and sometimes offered them support.

Mao calls a halt

Finally in the summer of 1968, faced with near civil war in various provinces, Mao decided to call a halt. Work teams were sent onto the campuses to restore order but were sometimes viciously attacked. Mao called a meeting of Red Guard leaders in the capital. Confronting their complaint that a 'Black Hand' was attempting to suppress the campus revolution, he announced that he himself was that Black Hand. Lin Biao, Zhou Enlai, Jiang Qing, Chen Boda, and Kang Sheng were all present to hear Mao effectively ending the Red Guard Movement.

Young people were ordered to lay down their arms, the army was empowered to deal with them by force if necessary, and the schools were told to prepare for the resumption of teaching. This still left the problem of urban youth now of school-leaving age who had missed two years of school. There were no jobs for them in the urban economy. A new programme began to send them to live and work in the countryside. In the following two years, five million young people were sent from the urban areas to be 'educated by the peasants'. Cadres and intellectuals were also sent to the villages to be re-educated in cadre schools, but while the majority of urban youth were exiled for the foreseeable future, the programme for most cadres and intellectuals became a rotating one in which they spent defined periods in the countryside before returning to their posts. Arbitrary arrest, imprisonment, and execution continued at a very high rate as the new revolutionary committees cracked down on civil disorder and on those deemed to have done wrong in the earlier years of the Cultural Revolution.

In October 1968 when the Twelfth Central Committee plenum was held to prepare for the Ninth Party Congress, so many of the original members had been purged that a quorum was obtained only by an unconstitutional action—Mao simply appointed an extra ten members. The meeting finally expelled Liu Shaoqi from the Party on the basis of a string of absurd charges. However, Mao rejected suggestions from the Cultural Revolution Group that Deng Xiaoping should also be expelled and would not accept that moderate veterans such as Zhu De, Ye Jianying, Li Xiannian, and Chen Yun should be demoted. Indeed, Mao defended them with the assertion—disingenuous from him—that they had a right to express their opinions. When Liu Shaoqi learnt of his expulsion he became very ill. Afflicted with diabetes and later tuberculosis he was an invalid for the last two years of his life. In October 1969 he was evacuated to Kaifeng during a war scare. He developed pneumonia and died deprived of medical care or even proper bedding. His wife was not released from prison until 1979. Deng Xiaoping escaped comparatively lightly. He was sent to live in Jiangxi with his wife and worked in a vehicle parts factory until recalled to Beijing by Mao in 1973.

The Ninth Party Congress held in April 1969 was supposed to celebrate the victorious conclusion of the Cultural Revolution. The new Party constitution it adopted restored Mao Zedong Thought as the theoretical basis for action and described Lin Biao as Mao's successor and close comrade-in-arms (see Figure 12). Jiang Qing, and her radical Shanghai associates, Zhang Chunqiao, Yao Wenyuan, and Wang Hongwen, all became Politburo members, as did Lin Biao's wife Ye Qun. The radicals kept control of the Standing Committee of the Politburo. On the other hand, against the advice of the radicals, Mao retained some of the old moderates on the Central Committee and even on the Politburo. He also made two military commanders new members of the Politburo. He knew that if the Party was now to be rebuilt and the economy restored, the army had to be kept on side, a coalition of interests constructed, and competent people put in control.

12. Jiang Qing, Mao Zedong, Lin Biao, and Zhou Enlai during the Cultural Revolution

The army had emerged greatly strengthened from the years of chaos. Once Mao decided to end the chaos he was forced to rely on military support. There were now army men in the leadership of every government office and every enterprise in China. The radicals had consolidated their power in the Party hierarchy. However, they had been weakened by the decision to disband the Red Guards. They were divided among themselves. They had been catapulted to high office by Mao's need for new associates and their own willingness to indulge in sycophancy, but they lacked an independent power base. Zhou Enlai and the central government ministries appeared greatly weakened. Apart from Lin Biao and Mao himself, Zhou was the only veteran revolutionary leader to hold on to his position unharmed, but even he had come under great pressure and had been unable to save some of his subordinates. He was now charged with restoring the economy and the work of government, a daunting task when so many senior officials had been purged. Yet his underlying position was strong. Once Mao had decided on a return to order, Zhou's abilities, hard work, and loyalty would once more prove indispensable.

Mao was now 76 years old. His Cultural Revolution was claimed as a great victory. He had reclaimed the personal power that had diminished after the Great Leap Forward. Liu Shaoqi whom he had identified as his main enemy was dead and others who had opposed his ideas were vanquished. His ideals seemed once more in the ascendant. The collective economy, now established in the villages, was achieving a modest success. Schools and universities reopened after the Cultural Revolution with revised entry standards intended to favour peasants and workers. Syllabuses were truncated and made less academic. The expansion of rural health services reduced rural urban health inequalities. Mao's belief that medical training need only take two years was now to be put to the test. Manual workers were represented on the revolutionary committees that now managed, nominally at least, enterprises and government offices.

The costs were high. Millions had died or been humiliated. Mao had damaged the structure and standing of the party to which he had devoted so much of his life. The elevation of the army negated his own principle that the party must control the gun. Although agricultural production was surprisingly little affected, constant civil disruption had affected industrial production and the distribution systems all over China and the economy as a whole had stagnated. Mao's regime had lost prestige both at home and abroad.

Intriguingly, the horrors of the Cultural Revolution remain better known than those of the Great Leap Forward and are often made more of in critiques of Mao's record, yet if the two are compared, the Leap with its incomparably higher death toll was the greater human catastrophe. The difference is that the majority of those who died in the famine were peasants and quickly forgotten in the world outside their villages. The victims of the Cultural Revolution by contrast were educated people, intellectuals, officials, and Party leaders. Their sufferings were more visible, even at the time, and a number of the survivors would later write moving memoirs.

After the violent years of the Cultural Revolution, the idealism that had motivated many Chinese to work hard and to accept privations for the sake of the revolution and the progress it would bring was replaced in many cases by cynical or fearful compliance. Living standards were little higher than they had been a decade earlier. Housing was still more overcrowded. Life, even in the cities was rather dismal. The few films, operas, and plays produced, like the new literature, dealt exclusively with revolutionary themes. Jiang Qing's model operas were not popular enough to achieve full houses. Even Mao complained that China's film output was inadequate and dull.

Mao had long been concerned about the problem of the revolutionary succession. Now perhaps he despaired. He had destroyed his relationships with all his old comrades but appeared to have little respect for his new associates. He had abandoned the idea of relinquishing the reins of power in his lifetime. As an individual he himself was more isolated than ever. He lived separately from his wife with whom he was quarrelling again. His children were no longer at home. For company, he was more than ever dependent on his bodyguards, his medical team, and the attractive young women who as secretaries, nurses, and attendants supplied him with care and sexual services in his final years.

Chapter 7
Decline and death

Two extraordinary events brought drama to the last years of Mao's life. The first, in 1971, was the defection and death of his heir apparent, Lin Biao, and the second was the visit of President Nixon to Beijing in 1972. These events astonished even well-informed onlookers and explanations for them are still a matter of dispute.

Hostilities with the Soviet Union

The Soviet invasion of Czechoslovakia in the summer of 1968 was dubbed 'social imperialism' by China. Beijing was not of course sympathetic to Dubček's liberalizing regime but it condemned Moscow's outright claim to the right to interfere in the internal affairs of fraternal socialist countries, seeing it as a threat to China's own security. This concern was exacerbated in March 1969 by a major clash on the Sino-Soviet frontier. There had been minor incidents earlier but this battle on the Ussuri River boundary in which the Chinese suffered heavy casualties in the face of superior Soviet firepower was on a different scale. Mao warned of the need to prepare for war. He and his colleagues made use of talk of the external threat to demand unity and the end to factional fighting, but their fear was real.

A further incident in Xinjiang on China's north-west frontier in August and rumours that the Soviet Union was considering a 'surgical strike' against China triggered plans to evacuate city populations, disperse key industries, and dig air raid shelters. A huge tunnel network was constructed in Beijing, designed to shelter half the population. (It would much later be recycled into metro lines, underground shopping centres, parking, cheap housing, and an underground city museum.) War panic had not abated by the autumn, and in mid-October the decision was taken to evacuate the Chinese leadership from the capital. Mao went to Wuhan and Lin Biao to Suzhou. It was in this exercise that Liu Shaoqi, sick with tuberculosis, was sent to Kaifeng, where he died a month later from medical neglect.

On 17 October, Lin Biao drew up a directive putting China's forces on red alert. It was issued the next day and an enormously expensive military mobilization took place. Mao reacted with fury and quickly rescinded the order. It is not at all clear how such a clash arose. Lin Biao was an extremely cautious man who had not made a move or expressed an idea for years unless he was certain that Mao would approve. The order had been sent to Mao before it was issued to the armed forces. It is possible that Lin took Mao's lack of a response for agreement. Or perhaps he believed the alert was simply a logical extension of orders that he had received. Whatever the explanation, Mao's trust in Lin was on the ebb. The incident had illustrated that the control of the armed forces was, in a very real sense, in the hands of his heir. And Mao had observed long before, 'Political power grows out of the barrel of a gun.'

The mysterious fate of Lin Biao

After the 1969 Party Congress Mao became increasingly distrustful of Lin Biao for reasons that remain somewhat obscure but may relate to his concern that the PLA now held too much power. The new Politburo and its Standing Committee were split between Lin Biao's military faction and the radical group consisting of former Cultural Revolution Group members. One of these, Mao's ex-secretary, Chen Boda, soon transferred his allegiance to Lin Biao from the radicals, possibly because, as Mao's named heir, Lin seemed to promise a better future. Each group vied for Mao's approbation. In 1970, their rivalry came to a head over two issues.

The first was the problem of who would succeed Liu Shaoqi as head of state. Mao suggested that the largely formal post could be abolished, but Lin Biao repeatedly proposed that Mao be appointed. The Chairman, who hated the sort of protocol the position involved, refused it and suggested that if the post was to be retained at all, Lin himself should take it. Mao may have been angered by what he saw as a new attempt to make him retreat into an elder statesman role. He believed his 1959 withdrawal to the 'second line' had enabled his colleagues to ignore his opinions and he did not intend to make the same mistake again. According to another view, Mao's behaviour was still more devious. He had already decided to get rid of his close comrade-in-arms in order to reduce PLA influence. He therefore raised the issue of state chairman to entrap Lin Biao. Had Lin, as expected, tried to get the position for himself, he could have been accused of attempting to seize power.

The next bizarre dispute arose in the late summer, over the so-called 'genius issue'. The second plenum of the Ninth Central Committee was preparing a new CCP constitution and it was proposed to include the formulation that Mao had developed Marxism-Leninism 'with genius, creatively and comprehensively'. This hyperbole was easily recognizable; it came verbatim from Lin Biao's preface to the *Little Red Book*. Zhang Chunqiao, knowing that Mao had already vetoed the formulation the previous year, opposed its use in the constitution. The air force commander, Wu Faxian, interpreted this as a deliberate attack on Lin Biao. He accused Zhang of denying Mao's genius and thus denigrating Mao Zedong Thought.

Lin Biao's supporters raised both these issues at the 1970 plenum. They asserted that there were still representatives of the Liu Shaoqi line who wanted to deny Mao's genius in the Party. Although they did not name him, Zhang Chunqiao was clearly their target. Perhaps because he saw Zhang Chunqiao as an important ally in upholding the values of the Cultural Revolution, Mao was infuriated by this attack. Alternatively, it has been suggested that Mao may covertly have encouraged the attack on Zhang in order to obtain a pretext to move against Lin's faction. In the event, Mao first moved against Chen Boda, who had been the most outspoken on the genius issue and who was the weakest member of Lin's group. He denounced Chen as a false Marxist, an accusation made especially ironic by the fact that, as Mao's secretary, Chen is known to have edited and perhaps ghost-written some of his theoretical work in the 1940s.

Through the autumn and winter Mao's anger did not abate. He refused to meet Lin and rejected the self-criticism produced in Lin's name by his wife Ye Qun and three generals who were Lin's allies as wholly inadequate. No doubt fearing for his future, Lin became depressed and spent his time in seclusion away from Beijing. Lin's son Lin Liguo, an air force officer with some seniority, was more proactive. Together with some close friends he began to discuss the possibility of assassinating Mao. He wrote a bitter characterization of Mao in sharp contrast to the usual eulogies. It presumably reflects what he had heard from his father and indicates why the family resorted to flight:

> Today he uses this force to attack that force; tomorrow he uses that force to attack this force. Today he uses sweet words and honeyed talk to those whom he entices, and tomorrow he puts them to death for some fabricated crimes. Those who are his guests today will be his prisoners tomorrow. Looking back at the history of the past few decades, is there anyone whom he supported initially who has not finally received a political death sentence?...His former secretaries have either committed suicide or been arrested. His few

close comrades-in-arms or trusted aides have also been sent to prison by him…

On 12 September, possibly because rumours of an assassination attempt had got out, the Lin family were panicked into action. Lin Liguo decided that they should flee to Guangzhou to set up a rival power base. However, his sister reported on them. Lin Biao, his wife, and his son took off in a plane just before their pursuers could stop them. Probably to minimize their time in Chinese airspace, they made for the Mongolian border rather than flying south. Apparently, there might still have been time to shoot the plane down, but when asked by Zhou Enlai if he wanted this, Mao replied with uncharacteristic resignation using a Chinese proverb about accepting the inevitable, 'You can't stop the rain, or stop your mother remarrying, let them go.' Soon afterwards the plane mysteriously made an unsuccessful crash landing in Mongolia. All the occupants were killed.

A way now had to be found to explain what had happened. The official account released gradually over some weeks gave the bare details of an assassination plot and the fatal crash. The story was received with incredulity; indeed, presumably because of their doubts, the Russians even disinterred the bodies and took parts back to Moscow where they were able to confirm from old medical records that one body was really Lin's. Even today, all versions of this improbable drama seem unsatisfactory. Most reconstructions of events rely on the idea that Lin Biao was power hungry. Yet he is known to have hated the limelight and left the day-to-day affairs of office to his wife, Ye Qun, who frequently represented him at meetings. He was also in poor health, reclusive, and according to some sources a morphine addict.

After his death, Lin Biao became a non-person. His books, calligraphy, and even the Party constitution were collected up and destroyed to eradicate all traces of the man who had stood a respectful half pace behind Mao at so many rallies and meetings.

In Beijing's Qincheng prison copies of *The Little Red Book* were gathered in so that Lin's preface might be removed, leading politically shrewd detainees to guess that Mao's heir had fallen.

Mao made use of the Lin Biao affair to reduce the dominance of the PLA in the Party and government. Four senior generals close to Lin Biao were arrested and the military faction in the Politburo was removed. Over the next few years, military officers were gradually replaced by civilians at lower levels. However, Mao's own authority was also weakened by the affair. To shore up the administration, he allowed many veteran cadres who had been disgraced, demoted, or imprisoned in the Cultural Revolution to return to their posts. The fall of Lin Biao inevitably cast doubt on Mao's judgement and he was quietly ridiculed by some. How could the Chairman have made such a poor choice? To lose one successor (Liu Shaoqi) might seem like bad luck, but to find that two were traitors? Even those who had retained some idealism about the Cultural Revolution became cynical.

The US card

Meanwhile, there had been astonishing developments in China's foreign policy. After the Soviet invasion of Czechoslovakia, which Mao had dubbed social imperialist, he was inclined to see the Soviet Union as the main danger to China. This focused his attention on the international scene. In 1969 he summoned Chen Yi, Ye Jianying, and two other marshals back from the political wilderness to review international affairs and report back to him. Despite ongoing border incidents with the Soviet Union, the marshals cast doubt on the idea Moscow posed a real threat, suggesting that its focus was really the competition with the USA for control of Middle East oil. However, having noticed some slight relaxation of US hostility towards China, Chen Yi raised the possibility of 'playing the US card'. Mao was interested: he thought the Soviet threat could be neutralized, to some extent at least, by a détente with Washington. It seemed that the Americans wished to extricate themselves from Vietnam and to avoid entanglements in Asia in the future. In this situation the threat from the USA which had dominated Chinese foreign policy for so long would be removed. The idea took a long time to bear fruit. Cautious contacts were initiated at ambassadorial level in Poland and later with Pakistan acting as an intermediary. In April 1971, the US table tennis team visited China—the so-called ping pong diplomacy. In July, President Nixon's security adviser Henry Kissinger made a top secret trip, and in October, with US support, the UN finally voted that the People's Republic, not Taiwan, should occupy China's place in the UN. Détente culminated with Nixon's visit to China in February 1972 (see Figure 13). This revolution in China's foreign policy initiated by Mao and carried through by Zhou Enlai improved national security and reduced the need to spend on the armed forces but tended to weaken ideological faith.

For all that he had wished to be rid of his heir, Mao's health was affected by the shock of Lin Biao's flight. He became depressed and stayed in bed for days. His blood pressure shot up, his legs became puffy, and he developed the shuffle characteristic of his last years. At the beginning of 1972 he succumbed to a lung infection that almost proved fatal. He was obviously ill and upset when on 10 January he attended a memorial for the veteran revolutionary Chen Yi, still in pyjamas topped by a heavy greatcoat. Anxious not to seem too enfeebled, he practised standing up and sitting down for weeks before Nixon's visit. Despite such efforts his poor health made the succession issue pressing. Who could be trusted to carry on the cause of proletarian revolution?

The battle for Mao's favour

The remaining years of Mao's life were characterized by a battle for his trust and favour. In one camp were radicals like Jiang Qing, Zhang Chunqiao, Wang Hongwen, and Yao Wenyuan. These

13. Mao shakes hands with President Nixon, 1976

diehard defenders of the Cultural Revolution on which their reputations had been built opposed anything that seemed to negate it such as the rehabilitation of veteran cadres. In the other camp were the moderates, including Zhou Enlai and other veteran revolutionaries and cadres, who would pay lip-service to the achievements of the Cultural Revolution but who wished to get on with rebuilding the government and the economy.

Despite his poor health, Mao retained control over China's destiny and over his cowed and deferential colleagues to an extraordinary extent. He permitted less and less debate. After 1973 he ceased to attend Politburo meetings, yet other Party leaders, though they might attempt to manipulate Mao's opinions, never opposed his wishes once he had made them clear. Mao performed a sort of balancing act between these two camps. After Lin Biao's death he was forced to rely on Zhou Enlai's unmatched skills in building up the new civilian-led administration and restoring China's foreign relations to normalcy. Yet he did not trust his cautious pragmatic premier ideologically, and would never choose him as his heir. Under the understanding by which the two men had worked together for so long, Mao decided on the direction of policy and Zhou worked out how to implement it. He might seek to change Mao's direction slightly or to modify a policy, but in the last analysis he would not oppose Mao. In May 1972, Zhou was diagnosed with bladder cancer. As the news spread, those in the know realized that Zhou, although younger than Mao by five years, might not outlive him, especially as the Chairman, who distrusted surgery, at first refused permission for Zhou to have an operation. The radicals were cheered. They increasingly saw Zhou as an enemy and a threat to their ascendancy. In September 1972 their position was further strengthened by Mao's decision to transfer one of their number, Wang Hongwen, from Shanghai to Beijing to be groomed for power.

A lingering embarrassment was the 1969 Party constitution which had specifically named Lin Biao as Mao's successor. In order to eliminate this anomaly the Tenth Party Congress was held early, in August 1973. It was a triumph for the radicals. They dominated the meeting and achieved a majority on the new Politburo Standing Committee. Wang Hongwen was given a prominent role and even cast Mao's vote on his behalf when he was too frail to attend. The symbolism was not lost on anybody. Wang was being considered for the succession. His meteoric rise was probably resented even by his fellow radicals who were far senior to him.

Despite the radicals' dominance in the CCP hierarchy, at this stage the executive was basically run by Zhou Enlai and other pragmatists. To general astonishment, and to the horror of the radicals, in February 1973 Mao allowed Deng Xiaoping, once condemned as 'the number two capitalist roader', to come back to the capital. A month later, Mao approved his appointment as vice premier in charge of foreign affairs. In 1974, Mao upset the radicals again by sending Deng to speak at the United Nations. As Zhou Enlai became weaker, Mao allowed Deng to take over much of the work of the executive, where he achieved considerable success especially in managing the economy. Mao had probably wanted Wang Hongwen to work with Deng and benefit from the older man's talent and experience, but he soon realized that Wang was not worthy of his hopes. Wang, inexperienced and inept, proved incapable of building new political alliances, and stuck close to his fellow radicals, especially Jiang Qing. Mao compared the two men at the end of 1974, lamenting that Wang was not as politically astute as Deng.

Although the pragmatists gained ground in many spheres, the radicals continued to hold sway in the arts, education, and the media. They launched a series of campaigns against their opponents using blanket coverage in the newspapers, wall posters, and compulsory study sessions. First, in 1973, came the 'Campaign to criticize Lin Biao and Confucius', which made the absurd claim that Lin Biao had been a covert Confucian. From criticizing Confucius, the radicals moved to attacks on the misdeeds of the Duke of Zhou, a mythological statesman of the 11th century BC admired by Confucius for his loyalty and uprightness. The target all too obviously was Zhou Enlai who had sometimes been nicknamed Duke Zhou. This was followed by denunciations of present-day Confucians in the Party (Zhou and Deng). In 1975, Zhang Chunqiao and Jiang Qing orchestrated attacks on 'empiricism and unprincipled practicalism' aimed at Deng Xiaoping. Finally, in the winter of 1975–6, came another attack on Zhou in arcane denunciations of Song Jiang, the rebel peasant hero of the 16th-century novel *Water Margin*. Mao condemned Song Jiang for having 'capitulated and practised revisionism'. The unfortunate Zhou Enlai was deeply upset. Minutes before major cancer surgery, he asserted to Deng Xiaoping, Zhang Chunqiao, and other leaders in attendance, as well as to his wife, that he had always been loyal to the Party and was not a capitulationist.

Jiang Qing, like the others, was manoeuvring for personal power. The campaign to criticize Confucius saw the publication of a number of studies of China's past female rulers casting them in a favourable light. Earlier, in 1972, she had attempted to raise her profile by granting days of interviews to a young American scholar to whom she spoke of her life, her marriage, and her views of literature and art. She came across as vain, impetuous, and surprisingly lacking in circumspection. Indeed, as the meetings were arranged by Zhou Enlai, one might almost suspect that he had set a trap for her to walk into. Mao was apparently infuriated when he heard of the interviews and prevented the transcripts from being sent out of China. The book for which they formed the basis was nevertheless eventually published in the USA in 1977, but stories of what Jiang Qing had said about her taste in films and books were circulating in China several years earlier, in an apparent attempt to discredit her. In the last years before Mao's death, rumours of quarrels between him and Jiang were passed around in government offices. A story that in 1974 he had told her that he no longer wished to see her as she never listened to him was received with quiet glee.

Mao's role in the shadow boxing was complex. Why did he allow the attacks on Zhou, who for years had devoted his extraordinary abilities to trying to make Mao's visionary policies work and was now a dying man? Equally why allow attacks on Deng Xiaoping whom he had made senior vice premier and later asked to chair the Politburo? It seems that Mao recognized that none of the radicals could match Zhou and Deng in the conduct of day-to-day affairs or foreign relations. He knew also that the radicals lacked wide support in the Party. He was disappointed by Wang Hongwen's incompetence and worried by Jiang Qing's ambition. At the same time he suspected both the premier and Deng Xiaoping of ideological backsliding. His solution was to allow the radicals to snipe at them, sometimes even participating himself, while keeping the attacks within certain boundaries. From 1974 he also became impatient enough with the radicals to make biting remarks about their faults. He warned Jiang Qing and her associates that they were behaving like a Gang of Four and criticized them for factionalism.

Fading health

As Mao's physical decline progressed, the battle for the succession intensified. It was not general knowledge that he had heart trouble, still less that in 1974 he was diagnosed with motor neurone disease; indeed he himself believed his difficulty in swallowing was due only to laryngitis. His pathetically infirm appearance in newsreels led to speculation that the nation was being prepared for his death. As he gradually lost muscle control due to the motor neurone disease, his face became contorted, he dribbled, and he needed help from his attendants to walk. Prominent among them was Zhang Yufeng, who had once worked on his special train and was later his mistress (see Figure 14). Prior to his cataract operation in August 1975 she read documents and papers to him. As he became frailer she nursed him, fed him, spoke for him, and even controlled access to him. In September 1975, Mao brought his nephew Mao Yuanxin, a supporter of the radical faction, to live in his residence to liaise between him and the Politburo. News of the outside world and in particular of Deng Xiaoping's activity now reached him through this filter. But even Mao Yuanxin needed Zhang Yufeng to interpret the grunts that had become Mao's sole means of communication.

Zhou Enlai died on 8 January 1976. The spontaneous outpouring of grief which followed caused such alarm that it was announced that there was to be no public mourning for him. The edict was widely disobeyed. People wore black armbands and white flowers and tens of thousands went to Tiananmen Square to lay wreaths. Although there had been no official announcement of the event, one million people lined the streets in the bitter cold of the evening to watch his cortège pass when he was taken to be cremated. Zhou Enlai was popularly regarded as standing for moderation and his death gave rise to deep unease. Deng's eulogy at the funeral

14. Jiang Qing and Zhang Yufeng (Mao's secretary/mistress), both wearing dresses designed by Jiang Qing and holding hands for the camera

praised Zhou for the qualities that people had so admired in the premier and that the radicals conspicuously lacked:

> [He was] good at uniting the mass of cadres, and upheld the unity and solidarity of the Party. He maintained broad and close ties with the masses and showed boundless warm-heartedness towards all comrades and the people.

On 3 February came the news that Mao had chosen a comparatively unknown official, Hua Guofeng, to replace Zhou as premier. There was shock that Deng Xiaoping had been passed over. In April, at the time of the Qing Ming festival when the Chinese remember their dead, mourners again flocked to Tiananmen to honour Zhou Enlai. They brought poems in his praise. Some even posted attacks on the radicals. The police emptied the Square with considerable force and there were hundreds of arrests. Mao gave his opinion that the disturbances had been 'a reactionary event'. Deng was blamed for fomenting them and stripped of all his posts although he retained his Party membership.

At the end of April, Hua, the new premier, had a rare interview with Mao who gave him a piece of paper in which he had scrawled, 'with you in charge I am at ease'. These six characters, written by an old man no longer able to speak comprehensibly, became Hua's claim to legitimacy as Mao's successor. Mao suffered a heart attack in May and a second one in late June. Marshal Zhu De died in early July and on 28 July a great earthquake in the industrial city of Tangshan killed a quarter of a million people. There was much talk of omens. Finally, on 9 September 1976, just after midnight, the feverish efforts of his doctors failed and Mao died. In China many reacted to the news with grief, some no doubt felt joy and hope; everyone was apprehensive.

Chapter 8
Legacies and assessments: the posthumous Mao

Mao's death immediately posed the problem with which he had tussled for so long: who would succeed him? Power first passed to Hua Guofeng, Mao's designated heir, who had been parachuted into the national leadership at the end of the Cultural Revolution. Foolishly, Jiang Qing and her radical clique had made no attempt to hide their resentment of Hua or to build an alliance with him. With the Chairman dead, they had lost their protector, yet they kept picking arguments with the new leader. They were later accused of preparing a coup. Whether this was true or not, Hua agreed with Marshal Ye Jianying and other surviving veterans to move against them. Ye's support brought military backing. Within a month of Mao's death, Jiang Qing, Zhang Chunqiao, Yao Wenyuan, and Wang Hongwen were arrested on charges of attempting to usurp Party and state power. The news was greeted with excitement and rejoicing on the street. Mao had once warned his wife and her associates that they were in danger of becoming known as the Gang of Four. This name was now used consistently to discredit them (see Figure 15).

Hua might arrest Mao's wife, but he still had to uphold Mao's reputation and continue the cult because his own legitimacy was

15. **The leadership line-up at Mao's funeral. In this official print, Jiang Qing, Zhang Chunqiao, Wang Hongwen, and Yao Wenyuan have been brushed out. However, no attempt is made to pretend they were not there. The gaps, of course, make it obvious and the characters of their names have been replaced with xxx or xx**

based on his claim to have been selected by the Chairman. Ignoring the Chinese leaders' agreement (originally proposed by Mao) that they should eschew the Soviet practice of preserving the body and instead be cremated, the Politburo decided to have Mao embalmed. A huge mausoleum was constructed in Tiananmen Square. Hua soon ordered that his own portrait should hang beside Mao's in public places and meeting rooms. In a move that was widely mocked, he even adopted a hairstyle that resembled Mao's. Prepared under Hua's direction, the fifth volume of Mao's selected works appeared in April 1977. To underline his loyalty, he announced a policy that became known as the 'two whatevers': 'Whatever policy Chairman Mao decided upon, we shall resolutely defend, and whatever instructions Chairman Mao gave we shall steadfastly obey.' At the height of his power, acting not only as prime minister but also as Party Chairman, and chair of the Military Affairs Committee, Hua enjoyed greater formal power than Mao himself had done.

Deng Xiaoping resurrected

Despite all this, the new leader's position was not secure. Deng Xiaoping began to lobby old friends to arrange his rehabilitation.

Former victims of Maoist political movements were naturally uneasy about the two whatevers policy. As a veteran revolutionary, Deng had an extensive network of support in the Party, the state apparatus, and the army. Those who had suffered in the Cultural Revolution could identify with him. He also enjoyed a reputation for competence and pragmatism. In the 1960s, justifying modifications to collective agriculture, he had famously said, 'No matter whether the cat is black or white, if it catches mice, it is a good cat.' This 'cat theory' had been repudiated in the *People's Daily* in 1967 and later the radicals repeatedly claimed it showed Deng lacked principle. Their attacks misfired because they made people associate Deng with a pragmatism that they saw as positive.

In April 1977 Deng wrote to Hua Guofeng admitting that he had made mistakes and promising that he would not try to reverse Mao's decisions. But in May he appeared to throw down the gauntlet to Hua by insisting that the 'two whatevers' policy did not accord with Marxism. He also pointed out that Mao himself had said that he was not infallible. Deng then out-manoeuvred Hua politically. In summer 1977 he was restored to his former posts and by the end of 1978 had effectively replaced Hua. Deng then began to put in place the range of new policies that became known as the 'economic reforms': incentive-driven household responsibility systems in agriculture, market mechanisms and incentives in the industrial and commercial sectors, and a general emphasis on expertise and technology. China's international trade increased rapidly and foreign investment was welcomed, cautiously at first, but as the years went by on an ever increasing scale. This new modernization drive was characterized by astonishing growth rates, improved living standards, rapid industrialization, and widespread privatization. It also involved the abandonment of the ideals of public ownership, collectivism, simple living, self-reliance, self-sacrifice, and egalitarianism promoted in Mao's China.

Reversing the verdicts

Deng now had to decide what to do about Mao's political legacy. The reassessment of Mao and the admission of his errors implied the reversal of verdicts on many of his victims. Tens of thousands of disgraced officials, teachers, and other professionals took up their old posts. Peng Zhen was restored to his post as secretary of the CCP Political and Legal Affairs Commission in 1980. Peng Dehuai, Liu Shaoqi, and many lesser names were posthumously rehabilitated. Released from prison in 1979, Liu's wife, Wang Guangmei, was appointed to the National People's Political Consultative Conference.

There remained the problem of the Gang of Four. Together with Chen Boda and five other surviving associates of Lin Biao they were put on trial in November 1980 accused of attempting to usurp power and of persecuting other communist leaders. The authorities were determined that the hearing should not be turned into a posthumous trial of Mao; a careful line had to be drawn between the late Chairman's errors and the defendants' crimes. Jiang Qing caused embarrassment by defiantly insisting that like an obedient dog she had done only what the Chairman wanted her to do. 'I bit those he wanted me to bite.' Zhang Chunqiao refused to speak. The others made confessions. Jiang Qing and Zhang Chunqiao received death sentences, later commuted to life, while Yao and Wang and the rest got long prison sentences. Ill with cancer, Jiang Qing committed suicide in hospital in 1991. Wang Hongwen died in prison in 1992. The other defendants including Zhang Chunqiao were eventually released.

Deng was ready to dump Mao's economic and social vision and wanted a complete disavowal of the Cultural Revolution. Yet, he would not countenance a total rejection of Mao's legacy, indeed he insisted, 'We will not do to Chairman Mao what Khrushchev did to Stalin.' Mao's own assessment of Stalin had been 70 percent merit, 30 per cent error. According to Deng, Mao once said that he would have been happy if such an evaluation had been made of his own work and indeed the 70/30 ratio is sometimes used in Chinese discussions of Mao's record. However, the official evaluation avoided the precision of a numerical rating. The 'Resolution on Certain Questions in the History of our Party since the Founding of the People's Republic of China' was approved by the Central Committee in June 1981, after much redrafting, and changes made by Deng himself, The key passage read:

> Comrade Mao Zedong was a great Marxist and a great proletarian revolutionary, strategist and theorist. It is true that he made gross mistakes during the 'cultural revolution', but, if we judge his activities as a whole, his contributions to the Chinese revolution far outweigh his mistakes. His merits are primary and his errors secondary. He rendered indelible meritorious service in founding and building up our Party and the Chinese People's Liberation Army, in winning victory for the cause of liberation of the Chinese people, in founding the People's Republic of China and in advancing our socialist cause.

Carefully, the resolution salvaged 'Mao Zedong Thought' by defining it as a theoretical synthesis of China's unique experience in revolution with the basic principles of Marxism-Leninism and as the crystallization of the collective wisdom of the Chinese Communist Party to which many other leading Party members had contributed. This system of ideas that constituted Mao Zedong Thought had to be distinguished from the mistakes Mao made in his later years. In a clear attack on the 'two whatevers', the resolution stated that it would be wrong to regard whatever Mao said as the immutable truth. However, it averred that 'Mao Zedong Thought will be the Party's guide to action for a long time to come'. As if to demonstrate the continuing respect to be accorded to Mao's works, a considerable number of Mao quotations were used to make points in the resolution. On the Cultural Revolution the resolution was unambiguous:

> Chief responsibility for the grave 'Left' error of the 'cultural revolution', an error comprehensive in magnitude and protracted in duration, does indeed lie with Comrade Mao Zedong...[he] imagined that his theory and practice were Marxist and that they were essential for the consolidation of the dictatorship of the proletariat. Herein lies his tragedy.

The veteran party leader and economic planner Chen Yun, who had clashed with Mao over the Great Leap, is said to have been more succinct, 'Had Mao died in 1956, there would be no doubt that he was a great leader of the Chinese people... Had he died in 1966, his meritorious achievements would have been somewhat tarnished, but his overall record still very good. Since he actually died in 1976, there is nothing we can do.'

Remembering Mao

Later, especially in the 1990s, much serious academic work on Mao written for a small audience appeared in China. Those who were once brushed out of history were restored: for example Lin Biao, though never rehabilitated, was once more listed as one of China's ten marshals. At a more popular level, the heroic episodes and the more presentable parts of Mao's personal life were covered in memoirs and in biopics such as the 1995 film about Yang Kaihui. People are not much encouraged to remember the bad things about the past. The most extraordinary example of expurgation was perhaps an article that appeared in the China *Youth Daily* (26 October 2006). It was written by Mao's granddaughter, whose mother, Li Min, is the only one of He Zizhen's children definitely known to have survived. The granddaughter wrote of the Maos and the Lius as two happy families who had lived harmoniously in Zhonghanhai, their children growing up together. She revealed that in 2004, Wang Guangmei had organized a reunion of three generations of the two families in a Beijing restaurant. It was attended both by Li Min, and by Li Na (Jiang Qing's daughter). Neither Liu Shaoqi's dreadful death nor Wang Guangmei's long incarceration get a mention. The sentimental account concluded, 'The reunion of these two families who had such a special role in China's experience was of historical significance.'

Mao's influence in China has waned, or at least changed, across the decades since his death. The official view is now that he should still be revered as the founding father of the People's Republic. However, as China has reached the 'primary stage of socialism' and faces new and different problems completely unforeseen by Mao, it is asserted that his solutions are not relevant to current conditions. Surveys show that young people believe Mao to have been a great man and even the saviour of China, but know very little about him.

Mao's image is still used in a great variety of ways. His face is on Chinese banknotes, and his portrait still dominates Tiananmen Square, gazing out across that great symbolic space towards his mausoleum. Jokey kitsch in the form of key rings, cigarette lighters, and playing cards bearing the Chairman's likeness appeared in huge numbers in the 1990s. Along with memoirs of the Chairman and popular accounts of his life they sold by the million. This commercialized Mao cult uses the Chairman's image in a far less respectful way than it was treated during the Cultural Revolution. Yet an element of veneration remains. Taxi drivers hang Mao figures on their windscreens as good luck talismans, and pictures of Mao accompany the kitchen god on family altars. In sharp contrast with the commercialized cult, unofficial homage is still occasionally paid to Mao's ideas. Laid-off or striking workers, peasants protesting at the compulsory purchase of their land, and other losers in the process of economic reforms sometimes carry Mao's portrait on protest demonstrations expressing nostalgia for a more egalitarian past.

Mao's last legacies

If Mao's influence has metamorphosed within China, outside China it has faded. Mao and his followers claimed that Mao

Zedong Thought was relevant not only to China but also to the struggles of all the oppressed peoples of the world. For a time, Mao did have a considerable following outside China. Maoist splinter groups broke away from most of the world's communist parties after the Sino-Soviet split, curiously often calling themselves Maoist, although the terms Maoism and Maoist were officially rejected in China both before and after Mao's death. In developed countries these tended to be small fringe organizations. In some developing countries, notably in Cambodia, Peru, India, and Nepal, Maoist groups led insurrections inspired by Mao's theory of 'people's war' in which peasants in the 'semi-feudal semi-colonial' world could be mobilized for national liberation. In Cambodia and Peru these movements were ultimately discredited by terrible violence and bloodshed. In India, insurrections which consider themselves Maoist still enjoy some success. In Nepal, the Nepalese Communist Party (Maoist) abandoned what are usually understood as the basic principles of Mao's thought when it moved from armed struggle to winning an election in 2008 and participating in a parliamentary democracy.

Concern for the future of China and the revolution was a consistent theme in Mao's utterances, expressed more frequently as he grew older and realized that he would, as he put it, soon go to see Marx. In a 1957 address to Chinese students in Moscow he said:

> The world is yours, as well as ours, but in the last analysis, it is yours.... Our hope is placed on you. The world belongs to you. China's future belongs to you.

By the 1960s, Mao's perception that the Soviet Union had become revisionist, and that China was in danger of going the same way, made him more pessimistic about what would happen in the next generation. In both the Socialist Education Movement and the Cultural Revolution the strong emphasis on revolutionary renewal and educating revolutionary successors reflect his anxieties.

A popular Cultural Revolution song, sung by millions of young people, began, 'We are the communist successors…' Mao's desire to control what happened after his death also contributed to the peculiar vulnerability of his designated successors. Liu Shaoqi, Lin Biao, Wang Hongwen, and Deng Xiaoping all fell because Mao came to see them as inadequate, and feared they would not maintain China on a revolutionary path. In his last years his premonitions grew darker. Conscious that Jiang Qing was unpopular, he reminded her how privileged she was and asked what she would do after his death. In 1976 his last recorded remarks to the Politburo were, 'What will happen to the next generation if the revolution fails? There may be a foul wind and a rain of blood. How will you cope? Heaven only knows.'

Yet despite his obsession with the revolutionary succession and protecting the revolution from reversal, at some level Mao perhaps understood the absurdity of believing that he could influence the future, or even imagine what it would be like. In 1970, he told Edgar Snow that 'future events would be decided by future generations and in accordance with conditions we could not foresee…The youth of today would assess the work of the revolution in accordance with values of their own. A thousand years from now, all of us, even Marx, Engels and Lenin would probably appear rather ridiculous.'

How would Mao have judged China today? Much of what he feared has come to pass. Since Mao's death, perhaps in reaction to the grim experience of the last years of his chairmanship, the CCP has practised collective leadership and has managed regular leadership transitions. Leadership struggles have been partially hidden from view. But the post-Mao communist leadership is part of a wealthy and powerful elite whose lives are very different from those of the ordinary people. This privileged class maintains its position through its vastly superior access to resources, education, and health. The CCP still uses ideology rhetorically, to stake its claim to legitimacy, but the stunning success of the Chinese economy and an enduring fear of turmoil (a legacy of the Cultural Revolution) are more important to its hold on power. Society is extremely inegalitarian; corruption and nepotism are rife. Workers of the old state factories have been laid off, land is seized from the peasants for urban development with miserably inadequate compensation, young migrant workers toil for grotesquely long hours in poor conditions to produce goods for the world market. Conspicuous consumption and ambition have replaced austerity and self-sacrifice. The commercial reprocessing of Mao's image reflects a dismissal of most of what the Chairman stood for. The ideological Mao would surely have condemned the way China has developed. Yet there was also a nationalist Mao who from the time of the May Fourth Movement had longed to see China rich, powerful, and respected among nations. This Mao would perhaps have applauded China's success, been gladdened by its phenomenal economic growth, and gratified by the spectacle of developed countries vying for its investment funds.

Assessing Mao

When it comes to judging Mao, his biographers are deeply divided. He has been condemned utterly by some biographers as a Chinese Stalin with a taste for killing. Others, while recognizing that he showed no great concern for the ordeals of his colleagues or those he ruled over, argue that he rarely gave instructions for the elimination of his opponents, and the deaths for which he was responsible were a by-product of his single-minded pursuit of the transformation of China.

Mao's life and his character are difficult to sum up because he was a complex man who behaved in contradictory ways. He embraced an imported modernizing ideology yet remained profoundly Chinese in his outlook. He was an idealist who produced inspirational writings but was prepared to accept suffering and death on an unimaginable scale to achieve his aims. He was a despot who proclaimed that 'it is right to rebel'.

He was an ideologue who wrote poetry. Mao recognized the contradictory nature of his own character when he wrote he combined a 'kingly' disposition demanding to dominate and suborn, with a 'monkey spirit' that urged him to run riot and throw all into disorder. Henry Kissinger saw the kingly Mao, observing that he 'distilled raw concentrated willpower' and 'exuded in almost tangible form the overwhelming drive to prevail'. These qualities contributed to the survival of the communist forces during the period of armed struggle and their remarkable victory. Once China was united, however, they were often harmful. Mao used his immense prestige to intimidate his colleagues and get his own way. He became increasingly autocratic, refused to listen to those who disagreed with him, and stubbornly enforced bad decisions. He bears responsibility for the horrors of the famine brought about by the Great Leap Forward, and for the tardy response to it which produced a death toll of tens of millions. His increasing tendency to interpret any criticism as a challenge to his leadership so intimidated his colleagues that in his last years many feared to express opinions at all. His Cultural Revolution caused immense suffering and social and economic disruption, yet until his death all leaders had to pay tribute to its achievements.

Mao's linguistic legacy

Whether because Mao had a gift for a pithy turn of phrase, or because so many people had to study his works for so long, he has had an influence on the Chinese language. Sayings and terms attributed to Mao are familiar even in English although people may use them without knowing where they come from. Here are some examples:

A revolution is not a dinner party.

Political power grows out of the barrel of a gun.

> A single spark can start a prairie fire.
>
> All reactionaries are paper tigers.
>
> Dogma is less useful than dog shit.
>
> Seek truth from the facts.
>
> The east wind prevails over the west wind.
>
> Great Leap Forward
>
> Gang of Four
>
> Cultural Revolution
>
> The sugar-coated bullets of the bourgeoisie (corrupting luxuries)

Mao's 'monkey spirit' made him conspicuously different as a communist leader. His language, at least before editing, was lively and readable. He frequently attacked doctrine and stereotyped language. He professed adherence to Marxism but seemed to contest its fundamental tenets by his insistence on the revolutionary character of the peasantry. In the Cultural Revolution he challenged the basis of Marxism-Leninism by encouraging attacks on the Party. Those whom he intended to purge were at a disadvantage because his actions seemed so incredible they failed to read him correctly. In 1973, it was the turn of the radicals to be aghast when he brought Deng Xiaoping, once condemned as the number two capitalist roader, back into power. Mao's mercurial transformations and unpredictable moves left everyone who worked with him far behind. He was shrewd and unpredictable in political struggle and often defeated opponents by dissimulation or by hiding his hand in order to draw them into a trap. He knew how to make a strategic retreat without any intention of losing real control. In his essay 'A Single Spark can Start a Prairie Fire', Mao wrote 'The enemy advances, we retreat; the enemy camps, we harass; the enemy tires, we attack; the enemy retreats, we pursue.' He applied these tactics throughout his life in political struggle as well as military action.

The consequences of Mao's actions were inevitably in proportion to the prodigious power he exercised, and the enormous population he ruled over. As a unifier and modernizer his achievements were immense, but his errors caused appalling suffering on a scale that is difficult to grasp. His utopian dreams, his periodic refusal to engage with reality, his ruthlessness, and his determination to win imposed terrible suffering on the Chinese people and cost millions of them their lives. He was ready to accept huge costs because he believed that suffering and death were inevitable in the pursuit of his cause. Mao's revolution improved life for those who survived it, bringing the economic development, education, and modernization on which subsequent progress was built. It also reunified China and made the country a force to be reckoned with in the world. He left an indelible mark on history.

Timeline

26 December 1893 Birth of Mao Zedong.

1911	Qing dynasty falls. Mao enrols in Republican Army.
1912	Establishment of the Chinese Republic.
1913–18	Mao attends the Hunan Teachers College.
1918	Mao works in Beijing University Library.
1919	May Fourth demonstrations in Beijing.
1920	Mao appointed school head and marries Yang Kaihui.
1921	Foundation of Chinese Communist Party (CCP).
1923–7	United Front. Mao works in both Guomindang and CCP.
1925	Sun Yatsen dies.
1926	Northern Expedition.
1927	Chiang Kaishek massacres trade unionists and communists in Shanghai.
1927	Mao Zedong leads Autumn Harvest Uprising.
1928	Mao and Zhu De's forces join up in Jinggangshan. Mao starts to live with He Zizhen.
1931	Japan occupies north-east China.
1931–4	Jiangxi Soviet Republic, Mao largely in eclipse.
1934–5	Long March.
January 1935	Zunyi Conference.

1937–45	Sino-Japanese War.
1938	Mao marries Jiang Qing.
1945	Mao achieves formal pre-eminence at Seventh CCP Congress.
1946–9	Civil war.
1949	Mao proclaims establishment of People's Republic of China.
1953–7	First Five Year Plan, agricultural collectivization, nationalization of industry.
February 1956	Khrushchev denounces Stalin at 20th Soviet Party Congress.
1956–7	Hundred Flowers movement.
1957	Anti-rightist movement.
1958–61	Great Leap Forward followed by famine.
1959	Peng Dehuai criticizes Mao at Lushan conference.
1966	Cultural Revolution begins. Formation of Red Guards.
1967	Liu Shaoqi and Deng Xiaoping disgraced.
1968	Red Guards disbanded. Youth sent to the countryside.
1969	Mao announces the end of Cultural Revolution and Lin Biao officially designated Mao's successor at 9th CCP Congress.
1971	Kissinger visits Beijing. China recovers UN seat. Disgrace and death of Lin Biao.
1972	Nixon visits Beijing.
1973	Deng Xiaoping recalled to Beijing, becomes vice premier.
8 January 1976	Death of Zhou Enlai. He is succeeded as premier by Hua Guofeng.
April 1976	Anti-radical demonstrations in Tiananmen. Deng Xiaoping removed from office.
28 July	Tangshan earthquake.
9 September 1976	Death of Mao Zedong.
6 October 1976	Arrest of Gang of Four.

November 1978	Deng Xiaoping reasserts himself at 3rd plenum of 11th Central Committee. Economic reforms launched. Peng Dehuai rehabilitated.
1980	Liu Shaoqi rehabilitated. Trial of Gang of Four.
1981	Resolution on Party History details Mao's achievements and his errors.

References

Chapter 1: Becoming a revolutionary

Two camps: Snow, *Red Star*.

Mao's notes on Paulsen (1917–18): Schram, *Mao's Road*, vol. i, pp. 175–313. This quote, p. 238.

Eulogy (1919): Schram, *Mao's Road*, vol. i, pp. 419–420.

Articles on Miss Zhao (1919): Schram, *Mao's Road*, vol. i, pp. 421–49.

Hunanese self-government (1920): Schram, *Mao's Road*, vol. i, pp. 543–77.

Letter to Cai Hesen (1921): Schram, *Mao's Road*, vol. ii, pp. 35–6.

Chapter 2: Organizing peasant revolution

Self-study university (1921): Plans in Schram, *Mao's Road*, vol. ii, pp. 88–98.

Text of poem for Yang Kaihui (1923): Schram, *Mao's Road*, vol. ii, pp. 195–196.

Report on Hunan Peasant Movement (1927): Schram, *Mao's Road*, vol. ii, pp. 429–64, or *SW* vol. i, pp. 23–55.

Analysis of classes (1926): Schram, *Mao's Road*, vol. ii, pp. 303–9, or *SW* vol. i, pp. 13–21.

Political power from a gun: 1927 citation, Schram, *Mao's Road*, vol. iii, pp. 31 and 36. 1938 citation, *Mao's Road*, vol. iv, p. 552, or *SW* vol. ii, 'Problems of War and Strategy' pp. 224–5.

Single spark (1930): Under this title in *SW* vol. i, pp. 117–28.

As 'Letter to Comrade Lin Biao' in Schram, *Mao's Road*, vol. iii, pp. 234–46.

Text of poem: Schram, *Mao Tse-tung*, Harmondsworth: Penguin, 1963, end pages.

Chapter 3: Yan'an

'On Practice' and 'On Contradiction' (1937): *SW* vol. i pp. 295–309 and 311–45. For the highly derivative lectures on which the essays are based see Schram, *Mao's Road*, vol. vi, pp. 617–827.

'My authority did not extend beyond my cave': Schram, *Mao's Road*, vol. vi, p. xl.

'Problems of Strategy in the Anti-Japanese Guerrilla War' (1938): *SW*, vol. ii, pp. 79–112 or Schram, *Mao's Road*, vol. vi, pp. 393–420.

'On Protracted War' (1938): *SW* vol. ii, pp. 113–94 or Schram, *Mao's Road*, vol. vi, pp. 319–89.

'The Question of Independence and Autonomy within the United Front' (1938): *SW* vol. ii, pp. 213–17 or Schram, *Mao's Road*, vol. vi, pp. 548–559.

'Problems of War and Strategy': *SW* vol. ii, pp. 219–35 or Schram, *Mao's Road*, vol. vi, pp. 548–59.

'On New Democracy' (1940): *SW* vol. ii, pp. 339–84 or Schram, *Mao's Road*, vol. vii, pp. 330–69.

'Reform our study' (1941): Schram, *Mao's Road*, vol. vii, pp. 747–54, or *SW* vol. iii, pp. 17–25.

Dogma less useful than dog shit: 'Reform in Learning, the Party and Literature', in Boyd Compton (ed.), *Mao's China: Party Reform Documents 1942-4*, Seattle: Washington University Press, 1952, p. 22. Entitled 'Rectify the Party's Style of Work' in cleaned up version in *SW* vol. iii, pp. 35–51.

'Yan'an Talks' (1942): *SW* vol. iii, pp. 69–98.

'Norman Bethune' (1939): *SW* vol. ii, pp. 337–8 or Schram, *Mao's Road*, vol. vii, pp. 312–13.

'Serve the People' (1944): *SW* vol. iii, pp. 177–8.

'The Old Man' (1945): *SW* vol. iii, pp. 271–4.

Ding Ling and Wang Shiwei's essays: Greg Benton and Alan Hunter (eds.), *Wild Lily, Prairie Fire*, Princeton: Princeton UP, 1995, pp. 69–82.

Liu's report (1949): Liu Shaoqi *SW*, Beijing: Foreign Languages Press, vol. i, pp. 314–64.

Chapter 4: First years of the People's Republic

'On the People's Democratic Dictatorship' (1949): *SW* vol. iv, pp. 411–24.

Mao's letters from the 1950s, in Kau and Leung (eds.).

Korean War: Chen Jian, *Mao's China and the Cold War*.

Mao, *Socialist Upsurge in the Chinese Countryside*, Beijing: Foreign Languages Press, 1956.

Mao's eulogy: Telegram on Stalin's Death: Kau and Leung (eds.), p. 327.

Mao on Stalin and agreement against personality cult: 'On the Question of Stalin' *The Polemic on the General Line*, Beijing: Foreign Languages Press, 1964.

First Chinese reaction to the secret speech: 'The Historical Experience of the Dictatorship of the Proletariat' *People's Daily*, 5 April 1956 in *The Polemic on the General Line*, Beijing: Foreign Languages Press, 1964.

'On the Correct Handling of Contradictions among the People (1957)': *SW* vol. v, pp. 384–421.

Deng Xiaoping's Report: *Deng SW* vol. 1, 1938–65, Beijing: Foreign Languages Press, 1992.

Eighth Congress Documents: Union Research Institute, *Documents of the CCP Central Committee 1956–1960*, Hong Kong, 1971.

Chapter 5: The Great Leap Forward and its aftershocks

Grain and procurement figures and industrial output: Carl Riskin, *China's Political Economy: The Quest for Development since 1949*, Oxford: Oxford University Press, 1987.

Mao's speech at Lushan Plenum: Schram (ed.), *Mao Zedong Unrehearsed*, p. 131.

Also at <http://www.marx2mao.com/Other/PGLtc.html>.

The atom bomb is a paper tiger: 'Talk with Anna Louise Strong', *SW* vol. iv, p. 10.

The nine letters: all reprinted in *The Polemic on the General Line*, Beijing: Foreign Languages Press, 1964.

Mao on personality cult: Edgar Snow, *The Long Revolution*, New York: Vintage Books, 1973, pp. 169 and 204–5.

Chapter 6: The Cultural Revolution: it's right to rebel

Mao, 'Directive on Public Health', 26 June 1965: Schram (ed.), *Mao Zedong Unrehearsed*, p. 232.

Bombard the Headquarters: MacFarquhar, Cheek, and Wu (eds.), p. 170.

Sixteen Point Decision: 'Decision Concerning the Great Proletarian Cultural Revolution'. 11th Plenum, 8th CCP Central Committee 8 August 1966. Schoenhals (ed.), p. 33.

'Mao's talk with Red Guards': 28 July 1968 accessible at <http://www.marxists.org/reference/archive/mao/selected-works/volume-9/mswv9_81.htm>.

Chapter 7: Decline and death

Lin Liguo on Mao and Mao on Lin Biao's flight: MacFarquhar and Schoenhals, p. 334.

Jiang Qing interviews: Roxane Witke, *Comrade Jiang Qing*, Boston: Little Brown and Co., 1977.

Mao no longer wished to see wife: Short, *Mao*, p. 614.

Mao warns about 'Gang of 4': MacFarquhar and Schoenhals, pp. 397–8.

Eulogy for Zhou Enlai: Ezra Vogel, *Deng Xiaoping and the Transformation of Modern China*, Cambridge, Mass.: The Belknap Press, 2011, p. 160.

Chapter 8: Legacies and assessments: the posthumous Mao

Agreement to be cremated: Answers to Italian journalist Oriana Fallaci, Deng Xiaoping, *SW*, vol. ii, Beijing: Foreign Languages Press, 1984, p. 331.

'Two whatevers': MacFarquhar and Schoenhals, p. 452.

'The Two Whatevers do not Accord with Marxism', *Deng SW*, vol. ii, Beijing: Foreign Languages Press, 1984, p. 51.

Mao not to be treated like Stalin: 'Answers to Fallaci', *Deng SW*, vol. ii, p. 329.

Resolution on Party history (1981): Text in Benton, vol. iv, pp. 91–137.

'Had Mao died in 1956': Roger Garside, *Coming Alive after Mao*, London: Deutsch, 1981, p. 206.

The world is yours: 'Talk at a Meeting with Chinese Students and Trainees in Moscow' 17 November 1957. Extract is in *Quotations from Chairman Mao*.

What will you do after I die?: Short, *Mao*, p. 614.

What will happen to the next generation?: Schoenhals, p. 293.

Mao's thoughts on the future: Edgar Snow, *The Long Revolution*, New York: Vintage Books, 1973, p. 222.

Jung Chang and Jon Halliday, *Mao: The Unknown Story*.

Philip Short, *Mao: A Life*.

The kingly monkey: Geremie Barmé, 'I am so Ronree' in Benton and Chun, p. 80.

Kissinger on Mao: Henry Kissinger, *The White House Years*, Boston: Little Brown and Co., 1979, p. 1058.

'Single spark' 1930: *SW* vol. i, p. 117.

Further reading

Bibliography

Delia Davin, 'Mao Zedong', in Tim Wright (ed.), *Oxford Bibliographies in Chinese Studies*. (New York: Oxford University Press, 2013).

Writing by Mao

Scholarly collections

Stuart Schram and Nancy Hodes (eds.), *Mao's Road to Power: Revolutionary Writings*, vols. i–vii (New York: M. E. Sharpe, 1992–2005). The definitive English-language collection of Mao's writing for 1912 to 1941. An invaluable work of scholarship which provides original texts and excellent historical introductions. For any texts that appeared in Mao's official *Selected Works* it indicates the edits made in Beijing after 1949 to sanitize the Chairman's work in the light of the politics of the time.

Stuart Schram, *The Political Thought of Mao Tse-tung* (Harmondsworth: Penguin, 1969).

Stuart Schram (ed.), *Mao Tse-tung Unrehearsed: Talk and Letters 1956–71* (Harmondsworth: Penguin, 1974).

Michael Y. M. Kau and John K. Leung (eds.), *The Writings of Mao Zedong 1949–1976*, 2 vols. (New York: M. E. Sharpe, 1986, 1992).

Roderick MacFarquhar, Timothy Cheek, and Eugene Wu (eds.), *The Secret Speeches of Chairman Mao: From the Hundred Flowers to the Great Leap Forward* (Cambridge, Mass.: Harvard Contemporary China series, 1989).

Official texts

Quotations from Chairman Mao Tse-tung (Beijing: Foreign Languages Press, 1967). A 'condensed Mao' carried by almost every Chinese during the Cultural Revolution and known in English as the *Little Red Book*. Available online at <http://www.marxists.org/reference/archive/mao/works/red-book/>.

SW: The Selected Works of Mao Tse-tung (Beijing: Foreign Languages Press; 4 volumes 1967, expanded 5-volume edition 1977). The 4-volume selection published in Beijing after 1949 is officially considered to constitute 'Mao Zedong Thought'. These texts can also be found online at the Mao Zedong Internet archive:

<http://www.marxists.org/reference/archive/mao/selected-works/index.htm>.

Biographies of Mao

Jung Chang and Jon Halliday, *Mao: The Unknown Story* (London: Random House, 2005). Best-selling, unremittingly hostile biography that was well received in the general press but heavily criticized by academic reviewers for its subjectivity and problematic referencing. A collection of reviews of this book appeared in Gregor Benton and Lin Chun, *Was Mao really a Monster? The Academic Response to Chang and Halliday's Mao: The Unknown Story* (London: Routledge, 2010).

Li Zhisui, *The Private Life of Chairman Mao* (New York: Random House, 1994). Gossipy memoirs by Mao's doctor.

Michael Lynch, *Mao* (London: Routledge, 2004). Focuses on the historical background to Mao's thought and career.

Maurice Meisner, *Mao Zedong: A Political and Intellectual Portrait* (Cambridge: Polity Press, 2007). Focuses on Mao's 'sinification of Marxism'.

Philip Short, *Mao: A Life* (New York: Henry Holt, 1999). Lengthy, thoroughly researched, and readable.

Edgar Snow, *Red Star over China* (London: Victor Gollancz, 1937). Famous account by the first western journalist to visit the communist areas. Includes Mao's own story of his life on which all subsequent accounts have to some extent been based.

Jonathan Spence, *Mao* (London: Weidenfeld and Nicholson, 1999). A short, accessible study that captures Mao's contradictory character.

Ross Terrill, *Mao: A Biography*, 2nd expanded edition (Palo Alto, Calif.: Stanford UP, 1999). Lively, detailed account by an author who also wrote a sensationalist biography of Jiang Qing (*The White-Boned Demon: A Biography of Madame Mao Zedong* (London: William Morrow and Co., 1984)). Both were best sellers in Chinese translation.

Studies on particular aspects of the Mao story

Geremie Barmé, *Shades of Mao: The Posthumous Cult of the Great Leader* (New York: M. E. Sharpe, 1996). A bittersweet look at the use of Mao as an icon.

Greg Benton (ed.), *Mao Zedong and the Chinese Revolution* (London: Routledge, 2008). A remarkable 4-volume collection bringing together reprints of significant articles on Mao from the previous forty years.

Timothy Cheek (ed.), *A Critical Introduction to Mao* (Cambridge: Cambridge University Press, 2010). An up-to-date overview. Fifteen scholars examine different aspects of Mao's life, thought, and influence.

Chen Jian, *Mao's China and the Cold War* (Chapel Hill, NC: University of North Carolina Press, 2001). An enlightening study of the interaction between Mao's domestic and international policies during the Cold War.

Gao Mobo, *The Battle for China's Past: Mao and the Cultural Revolution* (London: Pluto Press, 2008). A defence of Mao's record from a scholar who grew up in a Chinese peasant family.

Richard Kraus, *The Cultural Revolution: A Very Short Introduction* (Oxford: Oxford University Press, 2012). Useful brief read.

Simon Leys, *The Chairman's New Clothes: Mao and the Cultural Revolution* (London: Allen and Busby, 1977). Witty, bitter, and well informed.

Roderick MacFarquhar, *The Origins of the Cultural Revolution*, vols. 1–3 (London: Oxford University Press, 1974, 1983, and 1995). A well-researched trilogy which attempts to explain Mao's motives for launching the Cultural Revolution by examining the politics, economics, and international relations of China from the mid-1950s to the mid-1960s. Volume 3 is an outstanding work, of major importance to an understanding of Mao.

Roderick MacFarquhar and Michael Schoenhals, *Mao's Last Revolution* (Cambridge, Mass.: The Belknap Press, 2006). A detailed study of Mao's last two decades.

Michael Schoenhals (ed.), *China's Cultural Revolution: Not a Dinner Party 1966–9* (New York: M. E. Sharpe, 1996). An edited collection of documents with commentary.

General historical background

Rana Mitter, *Modern China: A Very Short Introduction* (Oxford: Oxford University Press, 2008).

Jonathan Spence, *The Search for Modern China* (New York: Norton, 1999). A comprehensive overview of China's modern history.

Websites

<http://www.marxists.org/reference/archive/>. Invaluable searchable site with links to works of Mao, Liu Shaoqi, Deng Xiaoping.

<www.morningsun.org/>. Site about Cultural Revolution.

<http://chineseposters.net/gallery/index.php>. Chinese propaganda posters including many of Mao.

Mao's train now in China's national railway museum is pictured at <http://www.theeastisred.com/trains.htm>.

Among the many websites showing Chairman Mao badges a tasteful collection is at <http://news.bbc.co.uk/1/shared/spl/hi/pop_ups/08/in_pictures_chairman_mao_badges/html/6.stm>.

Index

A

Agricultural policy 36–7, 55–6, 67–72, 113
Albania 75, 76
Anti-expert bias 68, 70
Anti-rightist movement 61–4, 70
Arranged marriage 5, 13, 24
Autumn Harvest Uprising 23

C

Cadre schools 92
Changsha 6–7, 12, 14, 17, 19, 27
Chen Boda 34, 83, 90, 92, 99–100, 114
Chen Duxiu 11, 14, 23
Chen Yi 102–3
Chen Yun 70, 93, 116
Chiang Kaishek 19, 22–3, 28, 32–4, 36
Civil War 1946–1949 45–7
Communist Party, Chinese (CCP) 2, 11, 15–20, 22–9, 32–40, 42, 45–6, 48–50, 57–65, 78, 81–2, 85, 99
 Congresses 15–18, 25, 27, 39–40, 64–5, 92–3, 105
Collectivization of agriculture 56–7
Comintern 15–18, 20, 22–3, 35
Confucius, campaign against 106
Cult of Mao 40, 78, 86–7, 117
Cult of personality/individual 60–1, 64–5, 78, 90, 117
Cultural Revolution 1, 21, 43, 78, 79–93, 95, 115–19, 121–2
Cultural Revolution Group 82, 92, 98
Czechoslovakia 97, 102

D

Deng Xiaoping 34, 63–5, 70, 73–4, 82–3, 90, 93, 105–10, 112–16, 118–19
Ding Ling 39
Dissidents 58–9

E

Economic reforms 113
Education reforms 56, 95

F

Famine 70, 74, 79, 95
First Five Year Plan 54–7
Futian incident 27

G

Gang of Four 108, 111, 114
Gao Gang 57
Genius issue 99
Great Leap Forward 65, 67–75, 79–80, 95, 121
Great Leap Forward, retreat from 73–5
Guangzhou Commune 23
Guerrilla tactics 26, 33, 35–6, 46
Guomindang (Nationalist Party) 2, 15–20, 22–3, 28–9, 32–3, 35, 43, 45–6, 67

H

Hai Rui Dismissed from Office 81
He Long 87
He Zizhen 25–9, 31, 40–1, 43, 77, 116
Health 3, 56, 79–80, 95
Hu Feng 59, 61
Hua Guofeng 110–13
Hunan Peasant Report 21
Hundred Flowers 61–4, 68
Hungarian uprising 1956 61–4

I

In Memory of Norman Bethune 38
Industrial growth and policy 55–7, 95, 113
Industrialization 49, 56, 63, 66–9, 113
Intellectuals 13, 16, 38, 49, 58–9, 61–4, 68, 86–7, 90, 92, 95

J

Japan 2, 7, 12, 28, 32–3
Japanese invasion 2, 32–3, 35–6, 38, 40, 43, 45

Jiang Qing 40–5, 52, 54–5, 77, 81, 83, 88–95, 103, 105–7, 111–12, 114, 119
Jiangxi Soviet 26–8

K

Kang Sheng 42–3, 83, 90, 92
Khrushchev 59–61, 66–7, 72–4, 76, 78, 80, 114
Kissinger, Henry 103, 121
Korean War 51–3

L

Land reform 26, 55–6
Lao She 87
Li Lisan 25–7
Liang Shuming 59
Lin Biao 26, 73, 78, 84, 92–4, 97–102, 104, 106, 116, 119
Lin Biao, death 97, 100–2
Lin Liguo 100–1
Little Red Book 21, 78, 86, 99, 102
Liu Dingyi 87
Liu Shaoqi 39–40, 57, 64–5, 70–1, 73–5, 82–4, 89–90, 93, 95, 98–100, 114, 116, 118
Living standards 2, 78, 95, 113
Lo Ruiqing 87
Long March 28–30
Lushan plenum 71–3, 77
Lüshunkou 45–6, 50

M

Mao Zedong
  assessment by Party after his death 115–16
  becomes leader of CCP 39–40
  brothers (Mao Zemin and Mao Zetan) 3–4, 25, 28, 52
  childhood reading 5
  children of 24–8, 40, 52, 54, 116

daughters (Li Min and Li Na) 43, 52, 54, 116
education 4–10
extended family 52–3
father (Mao Shunsheng) 3–5
health 108
mother (Wen Qimei) 3–4, 12
personal habits 43, 77
poetry 1, 18
political thought 1, 8–14, 34–3, 37–9, 40
sons (Mao Anqing and Mao Anying) 52–4
nephew (Mao Yuanxin) 52, 108
Selected Works 86
wives
 first wife 5
 second wife, *see* Yang Kaihui
 third wife, *see* He Zizhen
 fourth wife, *see* Jiang Qing
Maoism outside China 118
Marxism 14–16, 21–2, 34, 37, 64, 122
May 30th Incident 1925 19
May Fourth Movement 2, 11–12, 35
Mongolia 46
Moscow – Mao's visits 50–1, 66–7

N

Nanchang Uprising 23
New Fourth Army 36
New Youth 11, 14
Nie Yuanzi 83
Nixon, Richard 96, 103–4
North Korea 51
Nuclear weapons 66–7, 75–6, 85

O

On New Democracy 35, 37, 59
On the Correct Handling of Contradictions 62
On the Historical Experience of the Dictatorship of the Proletariat 60
On the People's Democratic Dictatorship 49

P

Peasant Associations 19, 23, 58
Peasant support for CCP 46
Peasant cooperatives
Peasant Training Institute 19
Peasants 17, 19–22, 24–5, 36, 49, 55–7, 59, 67, 69–70, 72, 74–5, 80, 95, 117–18, 120, 122
Peng Dehuai 23, 27, 52–3, 65, 71–3, 77, 81, 84, 87, 114
Peng Zhen 81–2, 114
People's Communes 67–9
People's Liberation Army 46, 115
People's Republic of China – establishment 45–9
Poisonous weeds 61, 63
Poland 61, 103
Post-Mao leadership 96–116
Privatization 113

Q

Qing (Manchu) dynasty 2, 6–8

R

Rao Shushi 57
Rectification movement 37–40
Red Army 23–4, 26–7, 29, 31
Red Guards 21, 65, 73, 81, 83–90, 92
Red Star Over China 3
Reform Our Study 37
Resolution on Party History 39
Revolution of 1911 8

S

Serve the People 38
Shanghai Commune 88
Sino-Indian border dispute 67
Sino-Soviet split 60–1, 66–75, 80, 97, 118
Sixteen Points 85
Snow, Edgar 3, 5, 8, 40, 48, 78, 119
Socialist Education Movement 75, 84, 118
Socialist Upsurge in the Chinese Countryside 56
Soviet Union, relations with 32–3, 36, 45–6, 50–2, 59–62, 66–76, 97, 102
Stalin 15, 24, 32, 34, 45–6, 50, 57, 59–62, 114–15
Succession planning 96, 98–9, 108–10, 119
Sun Yatsen 15, 17, 19
Support for People's Republic 58

T

Taiwan 46, 49, 51–2, 58, 66–7, 103
The Foolish Old Man Who Moved the Mountains 38
Thought reform 58
Three in one committees 88, 91
Tibet 67
Treaty of Friendship, Alliance and Mutual Assistance 50–1
Two whatevers policy 112–13, 115

U

United Front 17–19, 22, 33–6
United Nations 51, 105
United States, relations with 50–1, 58, 66–7, 76, 97, 102–3

V

Vietnam War 76, 92, 103

W

Wang Shiwei 39
Wang Guangmei 89, 114, 116
Wang Hongwen 93, 103, 105–7, 111–12, 114, 119
Wang Ming 34–5, 39, 42
War with Japan 33–4, 36–7, 43–5
Women in China 12–13, 21, 24, 43, 68
Women's Federation 58
World War II 2, 36
Wu Faxian 99
Wu Han 81–2

Y

Yalta 45
Yan'an 31–40
Yan'an Talks on Art and Literature 38, 59
Yang Changji 10–11, 14, 59
Yang Kaihui 11, 14, 18, 25–7, 40, 52, 116
Yao Wenyuan 82–3, 93, 103, 111–12
Ye Jianying 88, 93, 102, 111
Ye Qun 93, 100–1
Young Pioneers 58
Youth League 58, 65, 84

Z

Zhang Chunqiao 83, 90, 93, 99–100, 103, 106, 111–12, 114
Zhang Guotao 29–30
Zhang Xueliang 32–3
Zhang Yufeng 108–9
Zhongnanhai 49, 52, 54, 77
Zhou Enlai 29, 32–3, 35, 37, 45, 57, 70, 73–4, 82, 92, 94, 101, 104–9
  death 108–9
Zhu De 23–25, 27, 30, 73, 87, 93, 110